Eyewitness
SOCCER

1930s French hair-oil advertisement

1905 match holder

1900s ball pumps

Jay Jay Okacha of Nigeria

1900s shin pads

1910s shin pads

1930s shin pads

Early 20th-century soccer stencils

1966 World Cup soccer ball

1930s painting of a goalkeeper

1998 World Cup soccer ball

Early 20th-century porcelain figure

Eyewitness

Early 20th-century porcelain figure

SOCCER

Written by
HUGH HORNBY

Photographed by
ANDY CRAWFORD

1912 soccer ball

DK Publishing, Inc.

19th-century jersey

1900s plaster figure

DK

LONDON, NEW YORK, MUNICH, MELBOURNE, AND DELHI

Project editor Louise Pritchard
Art editor Jill Plank
Assistant editor Annabel Blackledge
Assistant art editor Yolanda Belton
Managing art editor Sue Grabham
Senior managing art editor Julia Harris
Production Kate Oliver
Picture research Amanda Russell
DTP Designer Andrew O'Brien and Georgia Bryer

REVISED EDITION
Managing editor Andrew Macintyre
Managing art editor Jane Thomas
Senior editor Kitty Blount
Editor and reference compiler Sarah Phillips
Art editor Andrew Nash
Production Jenny Jacoby
Picture research Carolyn Clerkin
DTP Designer Siu Yin Ho
Consultant Mark Bushell

U.S. editors Elizabeth Hester, John Searcy
Publishing director Beth Sutinis
Art director Dirk Kaufman
U.S. DTP designer Milos Orlovic
U.S. production Chris Avgherinos, Ivor Parker

1925 Australian International shirt

1905 book cover image

Early 20th-century snap card

This Eyewitness ® Guide has been conceived by
Dorling Kindersley Limited and Editions Gallimard

This edition published in the United States in 2005
by DK Publishing, Inc.
375 Hudson Street, New York, NY 10014

06 07 08 09 10 9 8 7 6 5 4 3

A catalog record for this book is
available from the Library of Congress.

ISBN-13: 978-0-7566-1091-3 ISBN-10: 0-7566-1091-5 (PLC)
ISBN-13: 978-0-7566-1092-0 ISBN-10: 0-7566-1092-3 (ALB)

Color reproduction by
Colourscan, Singapore
Printed in China by Toppan Printing Co.,
(Shenzhen) Ltd.

Discover more at
www.dk.com

1908 Newcastle shirt

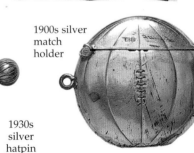

1900s silver match holder

1930s silver hatpin

1920s silver flint lighter

THE REFEREE

1940s whistle

Shirts from 1890s catalog

Contents

Hungary patch

Holland patch

Italy patch

Brazil patch

Early 20th-century child's rattle

1930s painted child's rattle

The global game

FOOTBALL HAS ITS ROOTS IN ancient China, Europe, and the Americas. People kicked a ball to prepare for war, to honour their gods, or just to entertain themselves. For centuries, different versions of ball-kicking games existed. In Europe, they were tests of courage and strength and in China and other Eastern countries, the games were rituals of grace and skill. The rules of the modern game of football were not drawn up until 1863 but the qualities that we admire in it – speed, agility, bravery, and spirit – have been present in many cultures for more than 2,000 years.

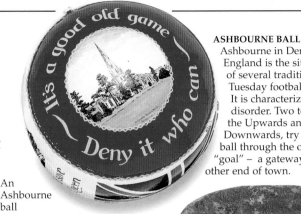

An Ashbourne ball

ASHBOURNE BALL
Ashbourne in Derbyshire, England, is the site of one of several traditional Shrove Tuesday football games. It is characterized by disorder. Two teams, the Upwards and the Downwards, try to move the ball through the opposition's "goal" – a gateway at the other end of town.

HARROW BALL
English public schools, including Harrow and Eton, played a crucial role in developing modern football in the early 1800s. Although each school played the game differently, they all produced detailed, written rules. These provided the basis for the first official laws.

The Harrow ball was flattened, top and bottom.

FOOTBALL TRAINING
The Chinese were playing a type of football by the 3rd century BC. A military book of that period refers to *tsu chu*, or "kicking a ball". The game may once have been part of a soldier's training and was later included in ceremonies on the emperor's birthday.

These symbols were once described by an official of the English Football Association as "To kick with the foot"

Chinese characters meaning "football"

A GENTLEMEN'S GAME
The game of calcio was played in Italian cities such as Venice and Florence in the 16th and 17th centuries. On certain festival days, two teams of gentlemen would attempt to force the ball through openings at either end of a city square. Although physical contact was a feature of calcio, the game also had a tactical element. Teams used formations and attempted to create space in which to advance.

Local people came out to watch the games

Handling the ball was part of the game

Players have to wear an elaborate costume of silk and gold brocade

Ball made from strips of leather

Men from many different backgrounds played football

STREET GAMES

This early 19th-century cartoon is subtitled "Dustmen, coalmen, gentlemen, and city clerks at murderous if democratic play". It shows the violent "every man for himself" spirit common to street games in Britain at that time. The damage done to property, particularly windows, and the disruption to the lives of other citizens caused many town councils to ban football – without much success.

ANCIENT RITUAL

The Japanese game of kemari probably developed in the 7th century from an ancient Chinese football game, after contact was made between the two countries. In contrast to the chaotic early football brawls of Europe, it involved many rituals and was played as part of a ceremony. The game is still played today and involves keeping the ball in the air inside a small court.

Kemari is a game of balance and skill

FOOTBALL WRITING

Football has been a popular literary subject for as long as the game has been played. The first-known book devoted to football is *Discourse on calcio* by Giovanni da Bardi, published in 1580 in Florence, Italy. Football has inspired poetry too. "A Match at Football" by Matthew Concanen was published in an anthology in the 18th century. The popularity of football increased rapidly in the early 20th century. *The School Across the Road* by Desmond Coke is one of many children's books published at around that time.

16th-century discourse on football

18th-century anthology

The children's book *The School Across the Road*

Colour plates appear throughout the book

Image from a 19th-century watercolour on silk

History of soccer

THE GAME THAT HAS CAPTURED the imagination of people all over the world was developed in England and Scotland in the 19th century. Graduates of English private schools produced the first common set of rules and formed the Football Association (FA) in 1863. Things moved forward quickly. British administrators, merchants, and engineers took the game overseas, and people from other countries began to play soccer. The first International matches were followed by professional leagues and big competitions.

Lord Kinnaird once did a headstand after winning a Cup final.

CELEBRITY PLAYER
The first soccer players were amateurs. C.B. Fry, who played for the Corinthians in the late 1890s, was one of the first soccer celebrities. He was also a member of the England cricket team and held the world long-jump record.

Arnold Kirke Smith's cap

EXHIBITIONISM
Throughout the early years of the 20th century, British teams toured the world, introducing soccer to other countries by playing exhibition matches. This shield was presented to the Islington Corinthians in Japan, in 1937.

The English Three Lions motif was first used in 1872.

Arnold Kirke Smith's England shirt

The shirt is made of closely woven wool.

THE FIRST INTERNATIONAL
In November 1872, Scotland played England on a cricket field in Glasgow in the first International match. About 2,000 spectators watched a 0–0 draw. This shirt and cap were worn by Arnold Kirke Smith from Oxford University, who was a member of the England team.

MODERN RULES
Lord Kinnaird was president of the Football Association from 1890–1923, and was one of the amateurs who shaped the rules and structure of the modern game. Previously, he had played in nine of the first 12 FA Cup finals, winning five.

TALENTED TEAMS
The English Football League began in 1888. Its 12-team fixture program was inspired by baseball. This 1893 painting by Thomas Hemy shows two successful clubs of the 1890s: Aston Villa, who won the league five times, and Sunderland, "the team of all talents," who won three times.

THE UNRULY GAME
The first French soccer league, set up in 1894, was dominated by teams of Scottish emigrants, such as the White Rovers and Standard AC. French satirists were quick to refer to the game's reputation for unruliness. This 1900s French magazine, *Le Monde comique*, reflects this attitude toward the game.

In reality, women's uniforms were far less figure hugging.

A ball of exaggerated size

Bystanders often got caught up in the boisterous action.

Cover illustration entitled *Les Plaisirs du dimanche* (Sunday Pleasures)

N° 720   NOUVELLE PÉRIODE   PRIX : **10 CENTIMES**

LE MONDE COMIQUE
ILLUSTRÉ
JOURNAL HEBDOMADAIRE, 8, RUE SAINT-JOSEPH, 8, PARIS

Prix des Abonnements : Paris, un an, 6 fr. — Départements, un an, 8 fr. — Union postale, 10 fr. — Un Numéro par semaine

LES PLAISIRS DU DIMANCHE. — par DRANER

— Mille excuses, madame... je suis un peu myope.. je croyais lancer mon ballon

LADIES FIRST
Women's soccer started at the end of the 19th century. Teams such as the British Ladies' Club attracted large crowds. During World War I, men's and women's teams played against each other for charity. The first women's World Cup was held in China in 1991 and was won by the US.

FIFA patch

FORMING FIFA
By 1904, several countries, including France, Belgium, Denmark, the Netherlands, Spain, Sweden, and Switzerland, had their own administrators. They formed the world governing body, FIFA (Fédération Internationale de Football Associations). By 1939, more than 50 countries had joined.

This 1900s plaster figure is wearing shin pads that were typical of that time.

Ugandan batik

Each stamp shows a different US player.

US stamps produced for the 1994 World Cup

OUT OF AFRICA
Soccer spread through Africa from both ends of the continent. South Africa, with its European populations, was an obvious foothold and sent a touring party to South America in 1906. In 1923, Egypt, in North Africa, was the first African team to join FIFA.

AMERICAN SOCCER
Youth soccer is the most widely played sport in the US, for both boys and girls. The 1994 World Cup provided a big boost for Major League Soccer, which is bringing top-level professional games to a new audience. The US reached the semifinals of the very first World Cup in 1930.

Rules of the game

THE RULES OF A GAME should be brief and easy to understand. It is certain that soccer's success has been partly due to the simplicity of its Laws. Rules governing equipment, the field, foul play, and restarts have all survived the passage of time. Soccer has always been a free-flowing game. Stoppages can be avoided if the referee uses the advantage rule – allowing play to continue after a foul, provided that the right team still has the ball. The offside rule has always been a source of controversy in the game. The assistant referees must make split-second decisions about whether an attacker has strayed beyond the second-last defender at the moment the ball is played forward by one of his or her teammates. A player cannot be offside from a throw-in.

STAND BACK
This throw-in is illegal. The ball is held correctly in both hands, but the feet, though they are both on the ground as they should be, are over the line.

There have been goalposts since the early days of soccer but, until the crossbar was introduced in 1875, tape was stretched between them 8 ft (2.5 m) from the ground.

The penalty spot is 12 yd (11 m) from the goal line.

Goal kicks must be taken from within the 6-yd (5.5-m) box.

Players must not cross the half-way line until the ball is kicked off.

PENALTY
Penalties were introduced in 1891 as a punishment for foul play, such as tripping, pushing, or handball within 12 yd (11 m) of the goal. A player shoots at goal from the penalty spot with only the goalkeeper to beat. If the ball rebounds from the post or bar, the penalty taker cannot play it again before someone else has touched it.

FREE KICK
There are two types of free kick – direct and indirect. In an indirect free kick, awarded after an infringement of a rule, the ball must be touched by two players before a goal is scored. Direct free kicks are given after fouls, and the taker may score immediately. Opposing players must be at least 10 yd (9 m) away from the ball at a free kick.

CORNER
A corner kick is taken when the defending team puts the ball out of play behind their own goal-line. Corner kicks provide useful goal-scoring opportunities. The ball must be placed within the quadrant – a quarter circle with a radius of 1 yd (1 m) in the corner of the field. A goal can be scored directly from a corner kick.

FAKING FOULS
The amateur soccer players of the 19th century believed that all fouls were accidental and would have been horrified by the "professional foul," an offense deliberately committed to prevent an attack from developing. The game today is full of deliberate fouls. Some players also fake being fouled to win their team a free kick.

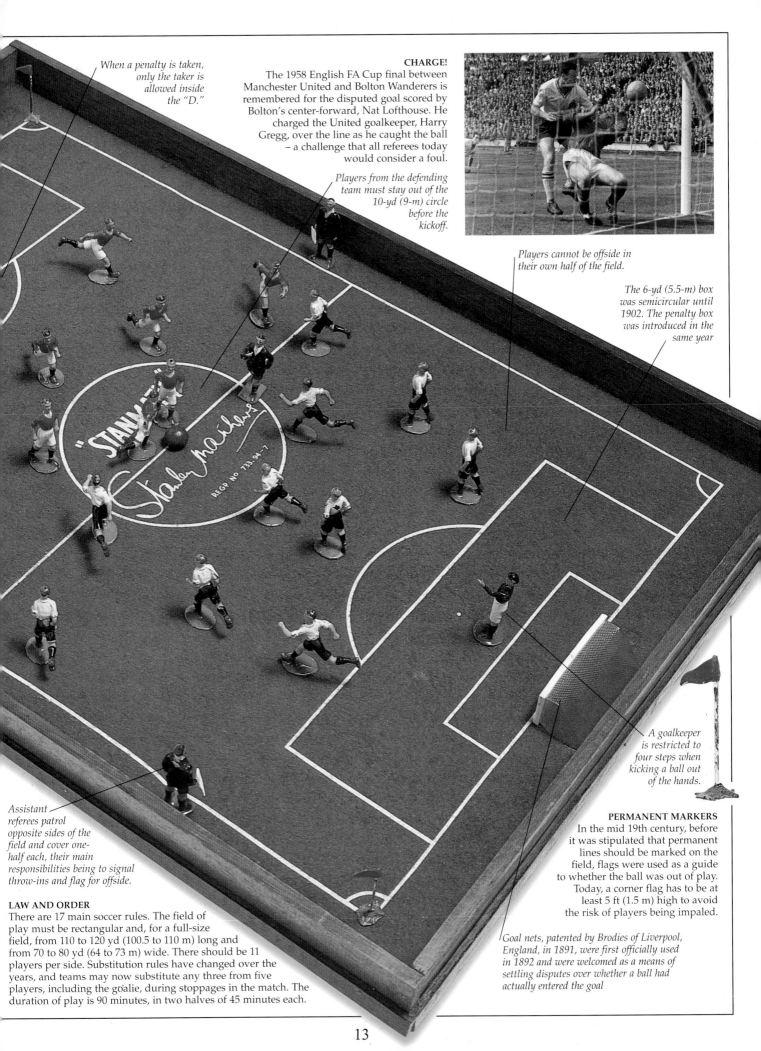

When a penalty is taken, only the taker is allowed inside the "D."

CHARGE!
The 1958 English FA Cup final between Manchester United and Bolton Wanderers is remembered for the disputed goal scored by Bolton's center-forward, Nat Lofthouse. He charged the United goalkeeper, Harry Gregg, over the line as he caught the ball – a challenge that all referees today would consider a foul.

Players from the defending team must stay out of the 10-yd (9-m) circle before the kickoff.

Players cannot be offside in their own half of the field.

The 6-yd (5.5-m) box was semicircular until 1902. The penalty box was introduced in the same year

A goalkeeper is restricted to four steps when kicking a ball out of the hands.

Assistant referees patrol opposite sides of the field and cover one-half each, their main responsibilities being to signal throw-ins and flag for offside.

LAW AND ORDER
There are 17 main soccer rules. The field of play must be rectangular and, for a full-size field, from 110 to 120 yd (100.5 to 110 m) long and from 70 to 80 yd (64 to 73 m) wide. There should be 11 players per side. Substitution rules have changed over the years, and teams may now substitute any three from five players, including the goalie, during stoppages in the match. The duration of play is 90 minutes, in two halves of 45 minutes each.

PERMANENT MARKERS
In the mid 19th century, before it was stipulated that permanent lines should be marked on the field, flags were used as a guide to whether the ball was out of play. Today, a corner flag has to be at least 5 ft (1.5 m) high to avoid the risk of players being impaled.

Goal nets, patented by Brodies of Liverpool, England, in 1891, were first officially used in 1892 and were welcomed as a means of settling disputes over whether a ball had actually entered the goal

The referee

Early 20th century caricature of a referee on a card for the game snap.

Early amateur players put a high value on fair play, but saw the need for officials on the soccer field. To begin with, each team provided an umpire from their own club, who didn't interfere much with the passage of play. At this stage, players had to raise an arm and appeal for a decision if they felt that they had been fouled; otherwise, play continued. The rise of professional football in the 1880s made it harder for umpires to be neutral. A referee was introduced to settle disputes. In 1891, the referee was moved on to the field of play and the umpires became linesmen, a system that has continued ever since. Linesmen and women, are now called assistant referees.

YOUR NUMBER'S UP
One duty of the assistant referees is to control the entrance of substitutes to the field, checking their cleats and indicating with number cards which player is to be replaced. At top levels of the game, a fourth official uses an illuminated board to indicate substitutes and inform everyone how much injury time will be played at the end of each half.

CLASSIC BLACK
This is the classic referee's uniform, all black with white cuffs and collar. Dating from the 1970s, it is similar to all those worn from the phasing out of the blazer in the 1940s to the introduction of other colors in the 1990s. The bulky jackets of the early 1900s were replaced by a less constricting shirt to encourage the officials to keep up with play on the field.

White trim sets off the all-black uniform

Notebook to record bookings, goals, expulsions, and substitutions

The yellow card is shown for bookable offenses.

Serious foul play results in a red card and expulsion.

1940s Acme whistle

Both sides of a FIFA Fair Play coin

Patch refers to the referee's local association.

Referees must look professional, with shirt tucked in at all times.

Referees may carry a handkerchief in case players get dirt in their eyes.

TOOLS OF THE TRADE
Certain items are vital to the referee's job. Red and yellow cards may seem like a long-established part of soccer, but they were introduced only in the 1970s. It is believed that the whistle was first used in 1878, and it was soon recognized as the best way of controlling play. Barrel-shaped whistles used to predominate, but other shapes are now common. The referee carries a notebook and pencil to record details of the match and a special coin that is tossed to decide which team kicks off and in which direction.

YOU'RE CARDED

Cards used to be given only once or twice per match, and expulsions were extremely rare, but FIFA now insists that referees be much stricter. As a result, teams regularly have to play with 10 team members or even fewer.

Cards are produced with a flourish from this pocket

The referee times the game with a watch.

The referee has to be fit to keep up with play on the field.

Former USSR

Australia

New Zealand

Bangladesh

Iceland

Portugal

USA

Columbia

Italy

WORLD-CLASS REFEREES

These badges are produced by Referees' Associations around the world. Despite all the abuse they receive, referees are motivated by the prospect of officiating at top-class games. World Cup matches are controlled by officials from all countries affiliated with FIFA, not just those that qualify as competitors.

LINESMAN FIFA 92

LINESWOMAN FIFA 95

Official FIFA patches for sewing on the officials' shirts

Men and women officiate at top-level soccer games.

TOUCHLINE HELPERS

The first linesmen waved a handkerchief to alert the referee. Assistant referees today use a flag. They wave the flag when a player is offside, when the ball is out of play, and when they have seen an infringement on the field.

The first referees wore plus-two trousers.

Blazer with pockets for a stopwatch and notebook

HOW TO BE A REFEREE

This illustration from the cover of a 1906 book entitled *How to Be a Referee* shows the typical referee's clothing of that period. After taking a qualifying exam, referees usually start out at amateur level. They are assessed regularly to ensure that standards remain high. Today's top referees are now professional. They earn good salaries for officiating top games.

The field

Patterns can be made when mowing the field

This Samuel Brandão painting of Rio de Janeiro shows football being played on bare earth.

At the start of a season, soccer players can look forward to playing their first game on a smooth green field. If a field is not looked after, it soon becomes muddy and uneven, especially if cold, wet weather sets in. Groundskeepers try to keep the fields in good condition with the help of new species of grass and good drainage. In many northern European countries, soccer takes a midwinter break during the worst conditions. Wealthy teams may lay completely new turf between matches, but millions of amateur players have to make do with whatever muddy or frozen land is available.

STREETS AHEAD
In the days before traffic became too heavy, street soccer was a popular pastime. Children learned close ball control and dribbling skills in confined spaces. They often used heaps of clothes or gateways as goalposts.

Groundskeepers preparing for a match during the 1953 English season

Jean-Pierre Papin playing for AC Milan, Italy, on a snow-covered field

PLAYING IN SNOW
In snowy weather, the field markings and the white soccer ball are hard to see and the ground is slippery. If the markings can be swept clear and the field is soft enough to take a cleat, soccer usually can be played, using a more visible orange ball.

HOT STUFF
In countries where the weather is cold during the soccer season, many methods have been tried to prevent fields from freezing. Underground heating was first installed in England at Everton in 1958. Before underground heating became common, groundskeepers put straw down as insulation and lit fires in braziers to raise the air temperature. Today, large covers are sometimes used to protect fields.

SLOPES AND SHADE
Modern fields are usually laid with a camber, which means that they slope slightly down from the center circle to the touchlines. This helps drain water away. When large stands are built, less air and light reach the grass, stunting its growth. This has been a problem at some stadiums, such as the San Siro in Milan, Italy.

Grass is kept long to encourage deep rooting.

Layer of topsoil nourishes the grass.

Heating pipes laid in grids.

Layers of sand and gravel allow water to filter away.

PAMPERING THE FIELD
Modern field maintenance is a full-time job. In the summer, the grass must be mowed, watered, and fed regularly. During the close season, work is done to repair holes and worn patches in the turf. New types of grass have been developed that grow better in the shade of tall stands. This is vital in helping the groundskeepers to keep the field in good condition.

The surface is made to mimic grass.

Fibers are woven together to form a carpet.

Artificial grass viewed from the side, top, and underneath

The base of the field is composed of large pieces of stone.

Drainage pipes carry water away.

Model of a section through a field

BETTER THAN THE REAL THING?
Some fields are made from synthetic turf laid on a shock-absorbent pad. They are more hard-wearing than grass fields and are unaffected by torrential rain or freezing cold. A team with a field of artificial grass can rent out its stadium for a range of events, such as pop concerts, and its home matches need never be postponed because of bad weather. Many players do not like the surface because they feel that it increases the risk of injury.

SATURATION POINT
Rainwater is the greatest threat to field condition. Good built-in drainage is therefore an important part of field construction. Pipes and materials chosen for their good draining qualities are laid under he grass. A large amount of sand is mixed into the topsoil to make it less absorbent and less prone to becoming waterlogged. Even a well-maintained field may become saturated. Groundskeepers sometimes have to use garden forks to remove standing water.

Soccer skills

Early 20th century button showing a man heading the ball

Each position on the field is associated with a specific range of tasks. Defenders must be able to tackle the opposition and claim the ball, midfielders need to pass the ball accurately to their teammates, and strikers have to shoot and score goals. Although most players specialize in a certain position, professional players are expected to master a range of skills and work on any weaknesses. As part of their daily training routine, they practice hard to perfect their skills so that their technique does not let them down in a game.

CONTROL FREAK
Some of the most gifted players, such as Brazil's Roberto Carlos, are able to manipulate the ball with their feet, making it swerve, curl, or dip. This type of ball control helps them bend passes around defenders and score from free-kicks well outside the penalty area.

Shouting helps the players pick one another out.

TACKLE TALK
Players try to take the ball from another player by tackling. Lilian Thuram of France and Parma, Italy, is one of the world's great tacklers. He shows the timing and precision that are essential to avoid committing a foul. Referees punish players if they make a physical challenge from behind or if they make contact with a player instead of the ball.

Lilian Thuram

Hand signals are used to improve teamwork.

Constant movement into space is essential.

PASS MARK
Moving the ball quickly around the pitch, from one player to another, is the most effective means of stretching a defence. Accurate passing remains the hallmark of all successful teams. Zinedine Zidane was the star of the 1998 World Cup final for France. He has the vision to pass the ball into space for his strikers even when he is tightly marked.

If the defender is unable to reach the ball, he must still challenge the striker.

The player must time his leap to meet the ball firmly.

Oliver Bierhoff

All parts of the foot are used to manipulate the ball in the desired direction

One-touch passing of the ball is the hardest to defend.

HEADS UP!
There are two distinct kinds of heading: defensive and attacking. Defenders try to gain distance when they clear a high ball out of the goal area. Attackers need accuracy and power to score goals with a header. Oliver Bierhoff of Germany, playing here for Milan, Italy, was an outstanding striker in the air.

The ability to pass with both feet gives the player more options.

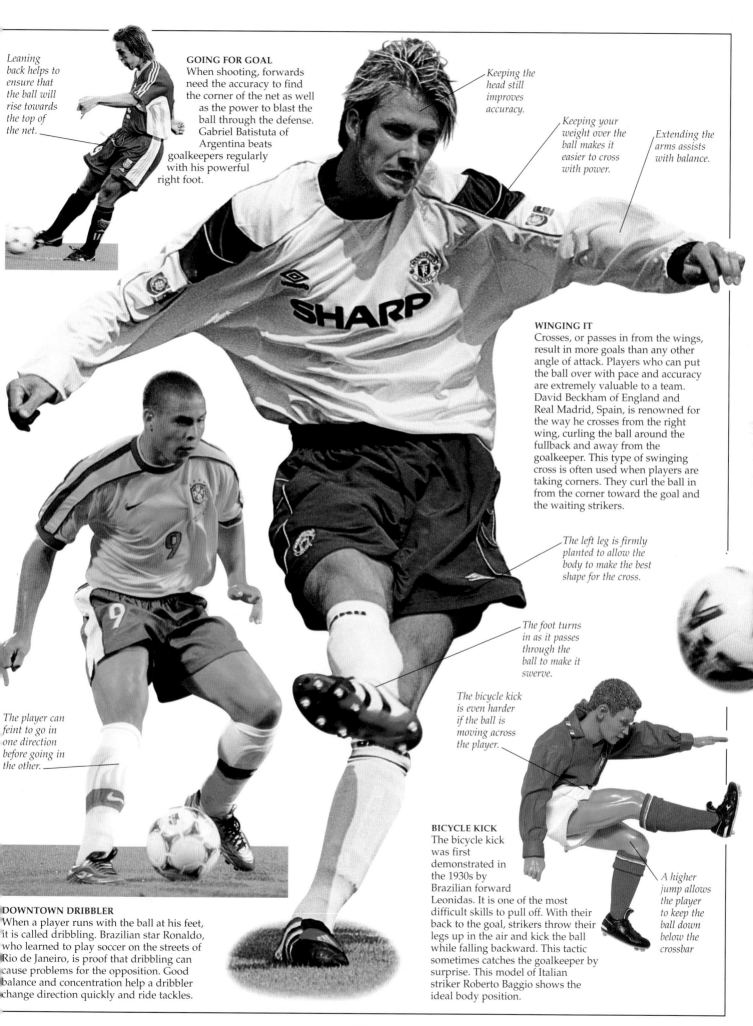

Leaning back helps to ensure that the ball will rise towards the top of the net.

GOING FOR GOAL

When shooting, forwards need the accuracy to find the corner of the net as well as the power to blast the ball through the defense. Gabriel Batistuta of Argentina beats goalkeepers regularly with his powerful right foot.

Keeping the head still improves accuracy.

Keeping your weight over the ball makes it easier to cross with power.

Extending the arms assists with balance.

WINGING IT

Crosses, or passes in from the wings, result in more goals than any other angle of attack. Players who can put the ball over with pace and accuracy are extremely valuable to a team. David Beckham of England and Real Madrid, Spain, is renowned for the way he crosses from the right wing, curling the ball around the fullback and away from the goalkeeper. This type of swinging cross is often used when players are taking corners. They curl the ball in from the corner toward the goal and the waiting strikers.

The left leg is firmly planted to allow the body to make the best shape for the cross.

The foot turns in as it passes through the ball to make it swerve.

The player can feint to go in one direction before going in the other.

The bicycle kick is even harder if the ball is moving across the player.

DOWNTOWN DRIBBLER

When a player runs with the ball at his feet, it is called dribbling. Brazilian star Ronaldo, who learned to play soccer on the streets of Rio de Janeiro, is proof that dribbling can cause problems for the opposition. Good balance and concentration help a dribbler change direction quickly and ride tackles.

BICYCLE KICK

The bicycle kick was first demonstrated in the 1930s by Brazilian forward Leonidas. It is one of the most difficult skills to pull off. With their back to the goal, strikers throw their legs up in the air and kick the ball while falling backward. This tactic sometimes catches the goalkeeper by surprise. This model of Italian striker Roberto Baggio shows the ideal body position.

A higher jump allows the player to keep the ball down below the crossbar

The goalkeeper

As THE LAST LINE of defense, a goalkeeper knows that a single mistake can cost the team victory. Goalkeeping can be a lonely job. It entails having different skills from the rest of the team, and you can be unoccupied for several minutes at a time. The recent change to the back-pass law, forcing the goalkeeper to kick clear rather than pick up the ball, has made the job even harder. The necessity of having both a physical presence and great agility means that goalkeepers have to train as hard as any other player, but the reward for this diligence can be a much longer career than that of their teammates.

A 1900s Vesta, or match holder, showing a goalkeeper punching clear

Clothes

Until 1909, goalkeepers were distinguishable only by their cap, making it difficult for the referee to judge who, in a goalmouth scramble, was handling the ball. From 1909 to the early 1990s, they wore a shirt of a single plain color that was different from the shirts worn by the rest of their team. A rule was made forbidding short sleeves but has now been relaxed.

GOOD SAVE
This 1950 comic cover shows the save that is considered to be the easiest to make – from a shot straight to the midriff. It also hints at the spectacular action in which goalkeepers are regularly involved, such as when they have to fly through the air to tip the ball away. Modern strikers are likely to make the ball swerve suddenly, so it is all the more important for goalies to keep their bodies in line with the ball.

CATCH IT
Punching the ball away from the danger area has always been popular among European and South American goalkeepers. The goalkeeper depicted on this 1900 book cover is trying to punch the ball, but he probably should be trying to catch it because he is not being closely challenged. In the modern game, referees rarely allow goalkeepers to be charged when they are attempting to catch the ball.

The ball should be punched out toward the wing.

KEEPERS' COLORS
Patterns in soccer shirts have traditionally been limited to stripes and rings, but since the rules on goalkeepers' clothes were relaxed, every combination of colors seems to have been tried. Not all of them have been easy on the eye, although fluorescent designs are easy for defenders to see.

The shamrock, symbol of Ireland

EIRE SHIRT
This shirt was worn by Alan Kelly for the Republic of Ireland. He made 47 appearances, the first against West Germany in 1957 and the last against Norway in 1973. Yellow shirts were once a common sight in international matches. Green was not an option for the Irish goalkeeper because the strip of the Irish team is green.

GOALIE'S GLOVES
Until the 1970s, gloves were worn only when it was wet, and they were made of thin cotton. Modern goalkeepers wear gloves in all conditions. Various coatings and pads are used to increase the gloves' grip, which is the key to handling the ball.

Flexible plastic ribs reinforce each finger

Modern gloves help to prevent injuries such as a broken finger.

NARROWING THE ANGLE

This image from the 1930s shows a goalkeeper alert to danger. When an attacker approaches the goal with the ball, goalkeepers should leave their line and move toward the ball to reduce the target area for the attacker. This "narrowing of the angle" is an important part of keepers' roles. They often make marks, in line with the posts, to help them keep their bearings when leaving the line.

Most goalkeepers may still wear a cap if the sun is in their eyes.

Arms are outstretched, ready to block a shot

THROWING OUT

This painted button from the 1900s shows one of the goalkeeper's jobs. A quick throw out, particularly after catching a corner, can be a way of launching an attack. Some goalkeepers are renowned for the length of their throw.

GOAL KICK

When the ball is put out behind the goal-line by an attacker, the opposing team is awarded a goal kick. The goalkeeper takes the kick from inside the 6-yd (5.5-m) box. Early leather balls absorbed water and increased in weight, so a goal kick rarely reached the opposition's half.

LOUD AND CLEAR

Peter Schmeichel is famous for the vehemence of his reaction when a team-mate makes a mistake. Here he is shouting at Roy Keane when playing for Manchester United, England. Although such eruptions risk undermining team spirit, it is far better for goalkeepers to communicate with their defenders than to be quiet. Goalies also have to shout when organizing the wall at free kicks.

Tactics

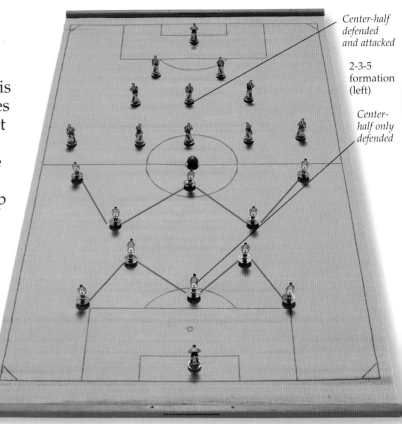

P ART OF SOCCER'S appeal is its tactical element. Coaches and managers try to outwit the opposition by keeping their tactics secret until the game. Since soccer first began, teams have lined up in different formations, trying to play in a way that will take their opponents by surprise and result in a goal. Early players had the physical attributes and skills needed for a particular position on the field. Today, the pace of the game demands that players be adaptable enough to play in almost any position, in the manner of the Dutch "total football" teams of the 1970s.

Old Arabic print of team formations

Center-half defended and attacked

2-3-5 formation (left)

Center-half only defended

W-M formation (right)

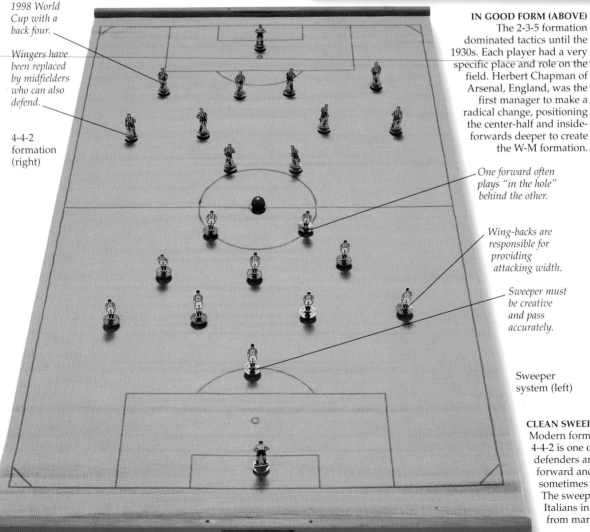

France won the 1998 World Cup with a back four.

Wingers have been replaced by midfielders who can also defend.

4-4-2 formation (right)

One forward often plays "in the hole" behind the other.

Wing-backs are responsible for providing attacking width.

Sweeper must be creative and pass accurately.

Sweeper system (left)

IN GOOD FORM (ABOVE)
The 2-3-5 formation dominated tactics until the 1930s. Each player had a very specific place and role on the field. Herbert Chapman of Arsenal, England, was the first manager to make a radical change, positioning the center-half and inside-forwards deeper to create the W-M formation.

GAME PLAN (ABOVE)
Managers use a board like this in the locker room. They employ it to show players how to counteract the opposition and where they should be at certain points in the game. This is particularly important when defending corners and free kicks.

CLEAN SWEEP
Modern formations are varied, but the 4-4-2 is one of the most popular. The four defenders are not expected to push forward and the four midfielders sometimes switch to a diamond shape. The sweeper system, perfected by the Italians in the 1960s, frees one player from marking duties to act as cover.

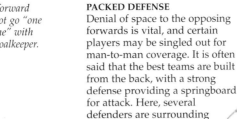

The forward cannot go "one on one" with the goalkeeper.

OFFSIDE ORIGINS

The first offside law, in 1866, stated that three defenders, including the goalkeeper, had to be between the attacker and the goal when the ball was being played forward by a teammate. By 1920, fewer and fewer goals were being scored because, even if attackers were onside at the vital point, they still had to beat the last outfield defender.

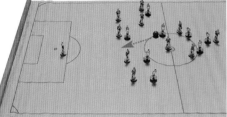

OFFSIDE UPDATED

In 1925, FIFA decided to amend the offside law so that only two players had to be between the attacker and the goal. Immediately, far more goals were scored. The offside rule is basically unchanged today. Here, the midfielder is about to pass the ball to the forward. This player is still onside and, once in possession of the ball, will have only the goalkeeper to beat.

Player is offside.

OFFSIDE TRAP

Teams without a sweeper, like Norway under Egil Olsen, are still able to use an offside trap. As the midfielder prepares to pass the ball forward, the defenders suddenly advance up the field in a line, leaving the forward offside when the ball is played. William McCracken of Newcastle, England, was famous for first perfecting this tactic, in the years before World War One.

PACKED DEFENSE

Denial of space to the opposing forwards is vital, and certain players may be singled out for man-to-man coverage. It is often said that the best teams are built from the back, with a strong defense providing a springboard for attack. Here, several defenders are surrounding a striker.

The attacker is trapped.

The defenders are physically blocking in the attacker.

NO SUBSTITUTE

Substitutions were first allowed by FIFA in 1923, but only if a player was injured. Injuries were faked so often to let coaches make tactical changes that it was gradually accepted that one player could be freely replaced. Now the number of substitutions allowed per team has increased to five for some games.

BE PREPARED

Javier Zanetti's goal for Argentina against England at France '98 was an example of how a well-rehearsed routine can work brilliantly. Lots of goals are scored from set pieces – movements that a team practices before a game. Coaches spend a great deal of time going through these with the team during training.

Injury time

A PROFESSIONAL SOCCER PLAYER'S job involves far more than playing games and enjoying the limelight. Training, fitness, and recovery from injuries are day-to-day concerns for the modern player. Advances in medicine mean that injuries that a few years ago would have led to inevitable retirement, can now be successfully treated. The pace of the modern game is unrelenting, and loss of fitness is likely to stop a player from staying at the top level. Physiotherapy, nutrition, and even psychology are all parts of the conditioning program of big teams today.

Mr Black the footballer from a Happy Families game

FIGHTING FIT
Medicine balls like this were used in soccer training for many decades. They are extremely heavy, so throwing them improves stamina and builds muscle bulk. Sophisticated gym equipment, training programs, and resistance machines are now commonly used. Strength and fitness are essential to success in the modern game because top players have to play as many as 70 games per season. The greatest players are superb athletes as much as they are skilled soccer players.

VITAL EDGE
Vittorio Pozzo, one of the first great managers, led Italy to victory in the World Cup in 1934 and 1938. He realized the importance of physical fitness and made his team train hard to give it a vital edge over its opponents. This paid off in extra time in the 1934 final, when Italy eventually scored the winning goal.

WARM UP AND COOL DOWN
A proper game-day routine can help prolong a player's soccer career. Modern players are aware of the importance of warming up thoroughly before a game. The risk of muscle tears and strains is significantly reduced if the muscles are warm and loose. Recovery after games is also important. Many players "warm down" after a match to relax their muscles before resting them.

The stretcher is carried by two wooden poles.

A pillow is built into the stretcher.

A piece of canvas supports the injured player.

GETTING CARRIED AWAY
This stretcher was used in the 1920s. In those days, if the stretcher was brought out on the field, the crowd knew that a player was seriously injured. Today, players are given a few moments to get up before they are carried off to prevent wasting time and delaying the game. They often resume shortly afterward. In the US, motorized buggies or carts have taken the place of traditional stretchers.

AS IF BY MAGIC
The "magic" sponge has a special place in soccer folklore. Spectators have often wondered how a rubdown with a sponge and cold water could result in a player's swift recovery from an injury. Today, the team physiotherapist, rather than the trainer, treats players for injury problems on and off the field. Physiotherapists are fully qualified to give sophisticated treatment to injured players.

The sponge is still used in amateur games.

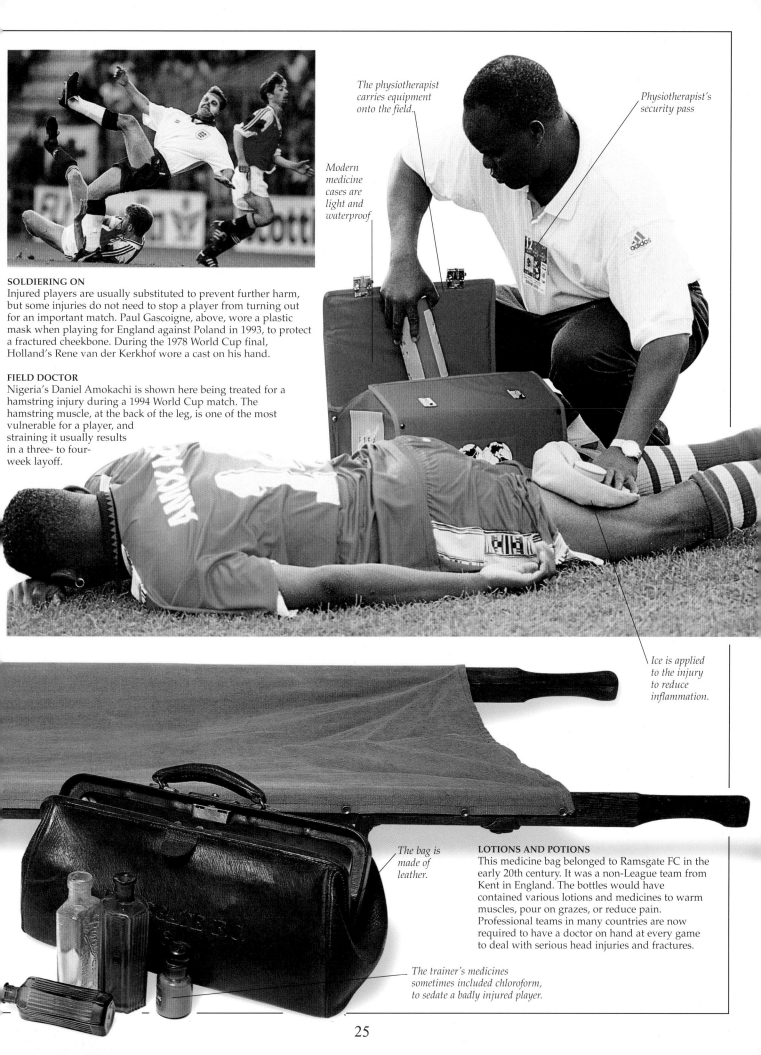

The physiotherapist carries equipment onto the field.

Physiotherapist's security pass

Modern medicine cases are light and waterproof

SOLDIERING ON

Injured players are usually substituted to prevent further harm, but some injuries do not need to stop a player from turning out for an important match. Paul Gascoigne, above, wore a plastic mask when playing for England against Poland in 1993, to protect a fractured cheekbone. During the 1978 World Cup final, Holland's Rene van der Kerkhof wore a cast on his hand.

FIELD DOCTOR

Nigeria's Daniel Amokachi is shown here being treated for a hamstring injury during a 1994 World Cup match. The hamstring muscle, at the back of the leg, is one of the most vulnerable for a player, and straining it usually results in a three- to four-week layoff.

Ice is applied to the injury to reduce inflammation.

The bag is made of leather.

LOTIONS AND POTIONS

This medicine bag belonged to Ramsgate FC in the early 20th century. It was a non-League team from Kent in England. The bottles would have contained various lotions and medicines to warm muscles, pour on grazes, or reduce pain. Professional teams in many countries are now required to have a doctor on hand at every game to deal with serious head injuries and fractures.

The trainer's medicines sometimes included chloroform, to sedate a badly injured player.

25

Soccer balls

MUCH OF THE APPEAL of soccer lies in the fact that it can be played without special equipment. Children everywhere know that a tin can, some bound-up rags, or a ball from a different sport entirely can be satisfyingly kicked around. This ingenuity was first displayed hundreds of years ago when people discovered that an animal's bladder could be inflated and knotted to provide a light, bouncy ball. A bladder alone did not last very long, so people began to protect the bladders in a shell made of animal skin cured to turn it into leather. This design worked so well that it is still used, but with modern, synthetic materials rather than animal products.

An 1890s brass traveling inkwell in the shape of a soccer ball

HEAVY GOING
Balls of the 1870s were often formed by stitching together eight segments of leather, the ends of which were secured by a central disc. The leather was unprotected and could absorb water on wet days, so that the ball increased in weight. Heading the ball could be dangerous, even fatal, and so this technique was not often used in those days. The dribbling game was the popular style, and the heavy ball was suitable for this style of play.

Manufacturers' names were first stencilled on balls in about 1900.

The lace for tightening the case is raised.

Interlocking panels of leather

Sections of leather sewn together

Tool for lacing the ball tightly

Copper stencil

MADE TO MEASURE
This ball was used in March 1912, in the international match between Wales and England in Wrexham, Wales; England won the match 2–0. Made from a pig's bladder wrapped in cowhide, it is typical of the type of ball used for most of the 20th century. The outside shell was laced up. The size and weight of soccer balls were standardized for the first FA Challenge Cup competition in 1872, but the balls still absorbed water and were prone to losing their shape.

The colors are based on those of the French flag

Brand name marked on the ball with a stencil

WORLD CUP COLORS
The first World Cup balls to have a color other than black were used in the Finals in France in 1998. They had a shiny, synthetic coating to make them waterproof and incorporated a layer of foam between the latex bladder and the polyester skin. This let players pass and shoot quickly and also put spin and swerve on the ball. Like 75 percent of the world's soccer balls, they were made in the Sialkot region of Pakistan.

HEADING FOR TROUBLE
Balls like this were used in the 1966 World Cup Finals, at which time ball design had hardly changed in 50 years. The leather case was backed with a lining, a development of the 1940s that improved durability. The outside was painted with a pigment that helped repel some water from a rain-soaked field. Manufacturers had still not found a reliable alternative to lacing up the ball, so players risked injury when they headed the ball.

The handle is pushed into the cylinder to pump up the bladder.

The piston expels air from the pump.

The Nesthill brass pump

The Sykometer measures air pressure.

Pump is used when standing upright.

Pressure valve

Pump from 1893 equipment catalog

Tube to attach the pump to the ball's valve

PATCHING THINGS UP
This 1970s repair kit would have been used with a vinyl ball. The metal rod was heated and then inserted into the puncture to create a hole of the right size, into which a patch could be glued.

Pump is inserted straight into the ball

Patch with "nipple" to fit the hole

Glue

Spare valve

Metal rod

BALL BOYS
This 17th century German engraving shows that inflated animal bladders have been used in ball games for a long time. The two men depicted are servants preparing a spare ball for their masters, who would have been playing pallone, a soccer game that was played in 17th century northern Europe.

1630 engraving made by Matthaus Merian the Older

FULL OF AIR
Over time, air escaped from a soccer ball's bladder, and a pump was used to reinflate it. Sometimes, the air pressure in a bladder was increased to improve the bounce of the ball. If a bladder was pumped up too high, it was likely to burst, so some pumps came with their own pressure gauge. These pumps date from about 1890.

Calcio balls are made of leather that is stitched together and then painted.

The use of two colors makes the Orkney ball flash in the air.

Alternative balls

Several different football games are played around the world. Each uses a ball particular to it. Some football games have existed for centuries. The balls may have features connected to a ceremonial aspect of the game, and involve decoration and color, or they may be designed to withstand harsh treatment. In some modern games the ball has evolved along with the game.

SHAPING UP
The game of football in the US was originally based on kicking a ball. As throwing became a central feature, the present shape of the ball evolved. The small ball can be gripped firmly, making it easier for the quarterback to make long, accurate passes.

BUILT TO LAST
In the Scottish Orkney Isles, a type of football game is played through the streets every New Year. The ball is much heavier than a normal soccer ball and is stuffed tightly with pieces of cork. This helps it last for several hours of play and allows it to float – a useful feature because a team can score a goal by throwing the ball into the sea.

MADE TO MATCH
Calcio, first played in Italy in the 16th century, was reintroduced to Florence in 1930. The game is played by teams of 27, all wearing medieval clothes and armor. Balls of various colors are used, including green, white, and red to match the costumes. Calcio balls are smaller than soccer balls, making it easier for the players to pick them up and throw them.

Soccer shoes

A 1950s painting of soccer shoes called *Christopher's Boots*, by Doris Brand

OF ALL SOCCER equipment, shoes have changed most over the past 100 years. Always the most expensive item of equipment, they remain an unaffordable luxury to many players around the world who have to play in bare feet. The fast, agile sport we see today would simply not be possible if soccer players had to use the heavy, cumbersome shoes worn up until the 1930s. Professionals then dreaded having to "break in" hard, new shoes, which involved a great deal of pain. They preferred to patch up an old pair again and again until they fell apart. In the first World Cup tournaments in the 1930s, the South American teams wore lighter, low-cut shoes, much to the astonishment of the Europeans. These began the trend toward the modern, high-tech boot.

MULTIPURPOSE SHOES
In the late 1800s, very few people playing soccer would have worn special footwear. These girl's shoes could also have been worn to school or in the house. The smooth soles, pronounced heel, and extremely high cut would have seriously constricted movement, but the ankle would have been well protected.

19th-century girls' shoes

1920s child's shoes

Playing soccer is a popular pastime with children.

MADE FOR THE JOB
By the 1920s, soccer shoes, like the "Manfield Hotspur," were being mass-produced for players of all ages. Children's shoes were designed just like adults', with reinforced toe caps and heels, some ankle protection, and leather cleats. Social conditions at the time, though, meant that most working-class families could not afford such equipment and, if they could, they would have handed down shoes from one child to another.

Extra foot support

Cotton laces

CLEATLESS SHOES
A 19th-century gentleman soccer player wore cleatless shoes, which would not have allowed for sharp turns or long passing. However, they were practical enough for the type of dribbling game favored by the great English amateur teams like the Corinthians. This style of play was dictated by the confined spaces used for soccer practice at many British private schools. Shoes like these would have doubled in weight when wet.

SHOES IN THE BATH
In 1910, these shoes were marketed as "Cup Final Specials," an early example of a soccer product being tied to a famous match. The wickerwork pattern on the toes was one of several designs that was thought to help a player control the ball – a major part of modern shoe design too. It was common for a player to wear a new pair of shoes in the bath for a few hours to soften the leather.

28

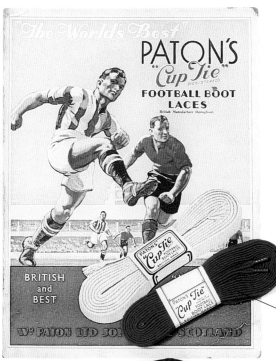

LOTS OF LACES
Paton's shoelaces, in various colors, were widely used from the 1930s onward. There was a constant demand for replacements because repeated soaking during matches, followed by drying out, caused the early cotton laces to perish and eventually snap.

PERSONALIZED SHOES
Shoes of a color other than black or brown are a feature of the modern game. Moustafa Hadji of Morocco was one of several players to wear a different color at the 1998 World Cup. However, this was not unknown in the past. Puma produced a white shoe in 1958, and England player Alan Ball was known for his white shoes a decade later.

Flexible ankle support

Laces were wrapped around the shoes for a closer fit.

White laces were common in the 1930s.

England's Tom Finney promoted these shoes

THE MODERN LOOK
The classic design of black with white trim, which is still used, began to be popular in the 1950s. The vertical strap on the instep remains from earlier designs. The shoes were becoming flexible enough to be worn without much breaking in. There was less protection around the ankle, which allowed players more freedom of movement but led to an increase in injuries. It was at this time that shoemakers began to use the name of famous players to sell their shoes.

THE DESIGNER AGE
A vast amount of money is spent on the research and development of modern shoes. Top-quality leather uppers, usually made from kangaroo hides, and light, synthetic soles combine to make shoes that last. They are comfortable and allow the best players to put amazing amounts of spin on the ball. Competition among manufacturers is intense, and huge amounts of money are spent on advertising.

Cleats are screwed into the sole.

Cleats and stuff

The number of cleats on the sole, and the way in which they are positioned, varies greatly. Longer cleats are needed if the field is wet and muddy; shorter ones are worn if the field is hard. The potential they have to cause injury has always been a concern to the game's governing bodies – in the 1930s, the wearing of illegal boots was an expulsion offense. Since 1900, one of the jobs of the referee or an assistant has been to check the cleats of every player entering the field of play. Anybody wearing shoes with sharp edges or protruding nails is not allowed to play.

Wooden hammer

Nails fixed to cleats

Separate nails

Key for tightening the cleats

THE FIRST CLEATS
Early soccer shoes were made entirely of leather. The cleats had to be hammered into the soles.

HARMFUL HAMMERS
Rubber cleats came next. They also needed nailing to the sole, and it was not long before the shoes were damaged.

ALL CHANGE!
Modern screw-in cleats are made of plastic or metal. Players can change their cleats at halftime, to adjust to changes in conditions.

Soccer uniforms

In the 19th century, both football and rugby players wore knee-length knickerbockers with no leg protection.

Shirts, shorts, and socks were described as the basis of a soccer uniform in the first rules of 1863, and they remain so today. The materials used for a soccer player's uniform have changed since then. Players in South America and Mediterranean countries needed clothing suitable for warm climates, so wool gave way to cotton and then artificial fibers. Cool fabrics that "breathe" are now the norm worldwide. Teams wear matching uniforms, or strips, on the field of play. The colors are the colors of the team, with which all the fans can identify. Most teams and International sides have a home and an away strip in case two teams wear the same colors.

DUTCH ORANGE
The Holland strip is unusual in being orange, and is recognized all around the world. The Dutch fans wear replica shirts and other orange clothes to form a mass of color at matches. Here, Marc Overmars is on the ball for Holland during the 1998 World Cup Finals.

WOOLLY SWEATERS
In the late 19th century, soccer jerseys were often made from wool. They tended to stretch out of shape and could become heavy in the rain because they soaked up water.

AWAY STRIP
In the 1966 World Cup final, the England team wore cotton shirts with a round collar. Although England was playing at home, they did not wear their normal white home strip because West Germany was wearing white. They wore red instead.

LACE-UPS
At all levels of the game, teams began to wear matching strips. This black-and-white shirt was worn by a member of Newcastle United's team for the 1908 English FA Cup final. Newcastle still wear black and white. The shirt is made of thick cotton with a lace-up collar. Lace-up collars became fashionable again in the 1990s and were worn by Manchester United, among other teams.

AUSTRALIAN AMATEURS
This Australian shirt is made from wool with a cotton collar. It was worn in 1925 by the player Tommy Traynor. Shirts worn in International matches have symbolic importance. At the end of the game, the teams swap shirts with each other in a gesture of goodwill.

KEEPING COOL
Today, most shirts are designed to keep players cool and draw away excess moisture. This 1994 Brazil World Cup shirt is made of light, synthetic fabrics. With the energetic pace of modern games, such improvements are vital, especially for matches played in hot climates.

FAIR-WEATHER FRIENDS
By the early 20th century, manufacturers in many countries had begun to adapt the kit that British players had taken overseas with them in the 19th century. They produced lighter clothes more suited to warm climates. Short-sleeved shirts and deep V-neck collars became part of the typical Mediterranean look, as represented on this image from Valencia in Spain.

These socks are unusually decorative.

Women were not expected to head the ball.

Early 1900s Spanish illustration

Hoops and stripes are classic design features.

PULL YOUR SOCKS UP
These socks from the 1920s look just the same as modern ones, but they are made of wool. Modern socks are made of synthetic materials, making them more comfortable. Players keep up their socks with ties or elastic around the top. The ties can be made from strips of bandage or elasticated tape cut up into lengths. Towards the end of a grueling match, when players are prone to cramp, they may discard the tie-ups. Socks around the ankle can be a tell-tale sign of a tired player facing defeat.

High kicking was easier if shorts were above the knees

Cream flannel shorts from about 1900

Modern synthetic shorts with decorative side seams

Hard-wearing cotton shorts from the 1930s

Early 20th century French illustration

UNDER WRAPS
Until World War I, women soccer players had to keep their hair under a cap and hide their legs inside voluminous bloomers. In the 1910s, when many men were away at war, crowds flocked to see women's exhibition matches. This wider acceptance of ladies' soccer enabled women's teams to start wearing soccer uniforms that were similar to those worn by men and more suitable for the game.

SHORT STORY
Amateurs in the 1860s played in long pants, but as the game developed, players had to increase their speed and agility. Shorter knickerbockers cut just above the knee became popular. The baggy style of soccer shorts of the 1930s was made famous by Alex James of Arsenal, England, "the wee man in the big shorts." This fashion was revived in the 1990s following a trend in the 1970s and 1980s for tight shorts.

Accessories

INJURY AND DISCOMFORT were part of the game of soccer in its early days. When protective equipment and other accessories, such as hats, earmuffs, and belts, were introduced at the end of the 19th century, they helped to distance the game from its rather violent past. Shin-pads were developed in 1874 by Nottingham Forest's Samuel Widdowson in response to the physical punishment that players suffered during games. Leg protection is still worn today, but other accessories are no longer used.

Catalog illustration of protective earmuffs

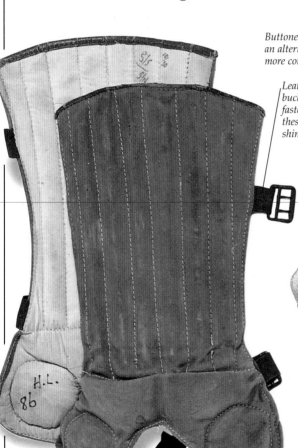

Buttoned tunic was an alternative to the more common shirt.

Leather buckles fasten these shinpads.

LASTING DESIGN
In the 1900s, players would have worn shinpads like these outside their socks, held in place with straps and buckles. The front section is made of leather and the back of cotton, with a stuffing of animal hair. This mix of materials was used in shinpads until the 1960s.

THE FIRST SHINPADS
The earliest shinpads were worn outside the socks and were extended to include ankle protectors, which rested on the top of the boot. Some, like these, had a suede covering, which was more prone to water damage than other types of leather. These heavy and inflexible pads date from the 1890s, about 20 years after shinpads became part of the soccer player's gear.

REINFORCED GUARDS
This figure is from a picture on the box of a late-19th-century German soccer game. His shin-pads, worn over the top of his socks and knickerbockers, appear to be strengthened with cane bars.

BELT UP
Decorative belts were a part of many youths' soccer gear until the 20th century. They spiffed up appearances by holding in the shirt and gave teams identity through the use of colors. Belts were also part of women's uniforms in the early 1900s.

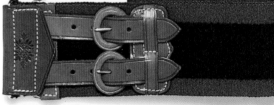

Early 20th century schoolboys' belts

Woman's belt from 1895

1980s shinpads were similar in shape to those from the 1930s.

Long laces to wrap around the leg twice

ROOM TO MOVE
By 1910, ankle protection was no longer part of shinpad design, not because it was not needed, but because it restricted movement of the foot. Passing and running off the ball had become important parts of the game, requiring increased flexibility of the ankle. Players were therefore forced to sacrifice some protection. Cork was sometimes used to strengthen pads.

TIE-ON SHINPADS
Shinpads worn inside the socks had taken over by 1930. Laces, instead of buckles, were used for fastening, to prevent chafing on the players' legs. Many years later, tighter-fitting synthetic, rather than woolen, socks held the pads firmly in position, without the need for ties of any sort.

LIGHTWEIGHT PROTECTION
Modern shinpads look dramatically different from earlier models. They are shaped to fit the leg, using lightweight materials to give excellent protection. Even the delicate Achilles tendon at the back of the ankle is shielded. The revival of ankle protectors, after a gap of 100 years, brings shinpad design full circle.

Women wore hats to keep long hair out of the mud.

KEEPING WARM
Gloves have become common, especially among players from hot countries, such as Brazil, who play in Europe, often in freezing temperatures. Players susceptible to hamstring and groin injuries are encouraged to wear Lycra shorts because they help to keep these important muscles warm.

Stripes to match team colors

Women's soccer hats

SOCCER PLAYER
This is a porcelain figure of a boy, made in the 1890s for export from Germany. Artistic depictions of soccer from this period often showed players wearing hats, even though they were becoming decorative rather than practical items.

Hand-painted German figure

Brazilian star Emerson

HATS OFF!
These women's hats date from 1895, when women's soccer was still in its infancy. The fact that women played in hats does not mean that theirs was a gentler game. Like the men, many women players wore shinpads for protection.

Famous players

SOCCER IS A TEAM GAME. Teams and national sides inspire the greatest passion among fans, but a few players are so gifted and entertaining that they stand out from their teammates and draw thousands of extra people to games. Some great players are famous for their spirit of fair play, while others have been surrounded by controversy and bad publicity. But all the great players share an ability to change the course of a game through a moment of incredible individual skill.

GORDON BANKS (b. 1937)
English goalkeeper Gordon Banks is remembered for one save in particular – a spectacular effort that kept out Pele's header in the 1970 World Cup. Banks won 73 caps between 1963 and 1972 and would have won more, but for an eye injury.

JOHANN CRUYFF (b. 1947)
One of the few great players also to have become a successful manager, Cruyff was able to instill in his teams some of the style and tactical awareness that made him such a joy to watch. He played for Holland, Ajax, and Barcelona, Spain. He personified the concept of "total football" by floating all over the field and using his amazing balance and skill to open up defenses.

GERD MULLER (b. 1945)
Known as "Der Bomber," Gerd Muller was an unlikely looking center-forward. He had an astonishing spring in his heels, which made up for his lack of height. He was a prolific goal scorer, with 68 goals in 62 games for West Germany. Most of his team soccer was played with Bayern Munich, Germany, for which he scored 365 goals.

Milla was a great entertainer, known for his flamboyant goal celebrations.

Roger Milla after scoring for Cameroon against Colombia in the 1990 World Cup

ROGER MILLA (b. 1952)
Twice African player of the year, Roger Milla of Cameroon was the first player to become famous worldwide playing for an African country. He was also the oldest player to appear and score in a World Cup final in 1994, aged 42.

BOBBY CHARLTON (b. 1937)
Manchester United star Bobby Charlton survived the Munich air crash that killed seven of his teammates in 1958. Known for the power and accuracy of his shooting, he was invaluable in England's 1966 World Cup win. He was knighted in 1994.

Eusebio practices ball control in training.

Eusebio scored 38 goals in 46 international games.

DIEGO MARADONA (b. 1960)
Maradona was the best player of his generation and one of the most controversial. He had a tremendous ability to inspire his teammates, most notably when leading Argentina to the 1986 World Cup and Napoli to two Serie A titles in Italy in the late 1980s. His magical left foot and strength in possession were his main assets.

Maradona's low center of gravity gave him excellent balance.

In the 1986 World Cup against England, Maradona scored two goals – one a handball that should have been nullified, the other a dazzling solo effort.

EUSEBIO (b. 1942)
Although he was born in Mozambique, Eusebio was snapped up by Benfica of Lisbon, Portugal, and went on to play for Portugal, as did several other talented players. He starred in the 1962 European Cup final, scoring twice as Benfica beat Real Madrid, Spain, 5–3. Eusebio was respected all over the world for his fair play and dignity as well as for his soccer talent.

Meazza (*below right*) shakes hands with Hungarian captain, Sarosi, before the 1938 World Cup final.

GIUSEPPE MEAZZA (b. 1910)
Italian Giuseppe Meazza won two World Cup winner's medals in 1934 and 1938. He was respected as a creator and scorer of goals from his inside-forward position. In 1938, he organized the Italian team when the coach, Pozzo, was ordered to leave the bench and sit in the stands. He spent his best years at Internazionale of Milan, Italy, and won 53 caps.

Like many of the greatest players, Maradona liked to be number 10.

GARRINCHA (b. 1933)
Nicknamed "the Little Bird," Garrincha had polio as a child. He overcame his disability to become one of the quickest and most elusive wingers the game has seen. He played on the right-hand side of Brazil's legendary 1958 forward line. In 1962, he made up for the absence of the injured Pele with some brilliant performances, helping Brazil retain the World Cup.

Maradona's magical footwork entertained and amazed the fans.

35

Continued on next page

MARCO VAN BASTEN (b. 1964)
Van Basten of Holland scored one of the greatest goals of all time at the European Championship final in 1988 – a volley from wide of the goal. Sadly, an ankle injury cut short his career.

LUIS SUAREZ (B. 1935)
Considered one of the best Spanish soccer players, Luis Suarez dominated the midfield for Barcelona, Spain, in the late 1950s. By the mid-1960s, he was playing a key part in Italian Inter Milan's new *catenaccio* system – a lineup heavy on defense with only two forward players. He was famous for his fast breaks out of defense and accurate passes. Suarez went on to be manager of Spain at the 1990 World Cup.

Kopa was the greatest French player of the 1950s.

Kopa was known for his careful ball control and well-thought-out passing.

Van Basten was the best center-forward of the late 1980s.

RAYMOND KOPA (b. 1931)
Creative midfielder Raymond Kopa made his name with the French team, Reims. He led them to the first European Cup final in 1956, where they lost to Spain's Real Madrid. Kopa played for France at the 1958 World Cup and was named European Footballer of the Year in 1959.

The two defenders are playing for the Italian team Roma.

Roma defenders are left in Platini's wake.

STANLEY MATTHEWS (b. 1915)
England's Stanley Matthews was known for his dribbling skills. One of his finest performances was in Blackpool's 4–3 win over Bolton in the 1953 English FA Cup final. He won 84 caps and played his last game for Stoke City at the age of 50. He was knighted in 1965.

LEV YASHIN (b. 1929)
Always outfitted in black, Lev Yashin was rivaled only by Gordon Banks as the greatest goalkeeper of his era. He played for the Soviet Union in three World Cups and is, to this day, the only goalkeeper to have been named European Footballer of the Year.

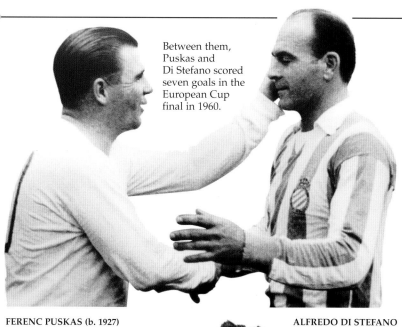

Between them, Puskas and Di Stefano scored seven goals in the European Cup final in 1960.

FRANZ BECKENBAUER (b. 1945)

Beckenbauer's intelligence shone on the field as he dictated play from a deep sweeper position. Together with Johann Cruyff, he is one of the few soccer-playing legends to achieve similar success as a manager. Having captained West Germany at the 1974 World Cup, he managed the team when it won again in 1990.

FERENC PUSKAS (b. 1927)

The star of Hungary's famous team of the 1950s, Ferenc Puskas was part of the Hungarian team that beat England 6–3 at Wembley in 1953. He joined Real Madrid of Spain in 1958. Puskas strongly favored his left foot, scoring a wealth of stunning goals for both club and country.

ALFREDO DI STEFANO (b. 1926)

When Real Madrid dominated European soccer in the 1950s, Di Stefano was one of its star players. His stamina enabled him to contribute all over the field. He and Puskas formed one of soccer's legendary double acts.

MICHEL PLATINI (b. 1955)

Platini was one of those players who seemed happy to take the weight of a nation's expectations on his shoulders. He captained France in the 1984 European Championships, and the team won the tournament for the first time. Platini was an attacking midfielder who often finished as top scorer at Italian club Juventus.

Michel Platini playing for Juventus

Platini had the speed and foresight to move forward into space

PELE (b. 1940)

Many people's choice of the greatest player of all would be Pele. He was king of Brazilian soccer from the late 1950s to early 1970s. He overcame constant fouling by frustrated defenders to score more than 1,000 goals for the Brazilian club Santos, American soccer team New York Cosmos, and the Brazilian national team. Despite being plagued by injury, his obvious love of playing and enthusiasm make him a perfect role model for the game of soccer.

Medals and caps

IT IS THE AIM OF ALL soccer players to play well and win each game. Those lucky enough to win a championship are awarded a medal as a mark of their achievement. Those good enough to be picked to play for their country win a cap. Medals and caps have been part of the game since the 19th century and are still valued rewards today. At the highest level, success can be measured by the number of caps a player has, and passing the "100 cap" mark is considered exceptional service to the national team. Thomas Ravelli of Sweden won 138 caps – a record for a European.

Argentine pot made from a dried eggplant trimmed with silver

Ornate silver dagger

Norwegian silver spoon

Argentine silver implement

Medals

As with military medals for soldiers, soccer players are rewarded with medals for helping their side, not for a moment of personal glory. Medals are awarded at all levels of soccer, professional and amateur. They are mementoes by which players can remember their glory days, and can become valuable collectors' items.

GOOD SPORT
Before organized leagues were established, soccer medals were often awarded for sportsmanship as well as victories. The full-back C. Duckworth was given this medal for "gentlemanly and successful play" in the 1883–84 season.

WITH COMPLIMENTS
This "complimentary medal for defeating all comers" in the 1884–85 season was awarded to B. Robinson of Accrington Stanley.

PRECIOUS GIFTS
As well as caps and medals, International players are sometimes presented with gifts by opposing soccer associations. The England team players received silver spoons when they faced Norway in 1949. The Argentine FA gave the England team members ceremonial daggers and other silver items on their first visit to Wembley, England, in 1951.

English v. Scottish League 1893

FA Cup runners-up 1893

DOUBLE
This group of medals belonged to R. H. Howarth of the Preston North End "Invincibles." The team won the League and the FA Cup in 1888–89, achieving the first English "double."

Lancashire Cup winners 1887

TROPHY TRIUMPH
This plaque was made to commemorate an International match between France and England in 1947. All the English players received a plaque after winning the match 3–0.

CLUB STRIKERS
Some clubs strike their own medals to mark a special achievement of their players. Preston North End awarded this one to their players for winning the English Second Division.

1909 Hungarian medal

CHAMPIONS
This medal was awarded to a player for success in the 1914-15 season.

AMATEUR
This 1920s medal was given to a successful amateur player.

ARSENAL STAR
This 1930s medal may have belonged to soccer star Alex James.

PLAY-OFF PRIZES
Medals have been presented to the winners of the third- and fourth-place play-off match at every World Cup Finals, except 1930 and 1950. At France '98, Croatia won third-place medals, defeating Holland 2–1 with goals from Robert Prosinecki and Davor Suker.

HUNGARY FOR SUCCESS
Hungary was one of the first European countries to take to soccer. The Hungarians copied the way other countries ran the game, including the awarding of medals. This medal was awarded to the members of an International team after a match against Austria in 1909.

Caps

A colored cap was once the only way of showing to which side a player belonged. In 1872, the FA ruled that teams should wear distinctive shirts. In 1886, it was suggested that caps be awarded to players each time they played for their country. Today, they are given to every member of a national team, including playing substitutes. Often, only one cap is awarded for a series of games, so a player with 50 "caps" has fewer actual ones.

HOME CAP
This Welsh cap was awarded for the 1903–04 Home International matches among England, Scotland, Northern Ireland, and Wales. This tournament took place every year until 1984.

CAREY'S CAP
The great defender Johnny Carey won this cap when he played for Ireland against Poland and Switzerland in 1938. Carey won 36 caps.

Tassels are added for decoration.

Welsh national crest – a dragon

Details of different matches can be embroidered into each panel.

Soccer caps are usually made of velvet.

SCHOOL COLORS
Soccer caps were first awarded in English private schools. "Colors," in the form of caps, were given to the most able players in each year.

IN TRAINING
It is not only players who are rewarded for their efforts. Trainer Will Scott received this medal when the English and Scottish Leagues met at Celtic Park, Glasgow, Scotland, in November 1931.

The date covers games from a whole season.

Northern Ireland had its own team from 1921.

WAR GAMES
Throughout World War II, famous International players took part in exhibition matches arranged to boost public morale. In 1946, Tom Finney was given this set of three medals after appearing in a match in Antwerp, Belgium.

PROMOTIONAL MEDAL
By the 1950s, businesses had started to commemorate a range of soccer events. The French newspaper *Le Soir* made this medal to mark a club tour of Austria in 1953.

WORLD CUP
The biggest achievement in soccer is to win the World Cup. This is a spare Jules Rimet medal from the 1954 final, when West Germany beat the favorites, Hungary.

AFRICAN CUP
This medal was presented to the winners of the first African Nations' Cup in 1957. The competition was held in Khartoum, Sudan, and only Sudan, Ethiopia, and Egypt took part. Egypt beat Ethiopia 4–0 in the final.

Famous teams

SOME TEAMS INSPIRE the greatest loyalty and passion from soccer fans, more so even than national teams. In every country, certain big teams attract followers from beyond their local areas and tend to dominate their domestic leagues and cups. Success for these teams often continues because financial backing ensures a steady supply of good new players. In all corners of the world, people swear allegiance to Barcelona or Liverpool, Flamengo or Milan, although they may never be able to attend a game involving their team.

ITALIAN ZEBRAS
Juventus is the most successful Italian team and enjoys great support outside Turin. Nicknamed the Zebras for its black-and-white striped shirt, Juventus won the European Cup in 1985 and 1996.

BRAVO BENFICA
Only Porto and Sporting Lisbon rival Benfica in the Portuguese League. Benfica also has had some notable victories on the more competitive European stage. Benfica was the great team of the early 1960s, winning two European Cups, in 1961 and 1962, and reaching but losing three further finals.

This bronze depicts Benfica's symbol, an eagle.

Figure of the ancient Greek hero Ajax forms the basis of the team's crest.

MIGHTY MARSEILLE
In 1993, Marseille, France, led by the attacking threat of Allen Boksic and Rudi Voller, beat AC Milan of Italy 1–0 to lift the European Cup. French administrators, such as long-time FIFA president Jules Rimet, have always had a large role in soccer, but it was 1993 before a French team won a European trophy.

LONDON LADIES
Netty Honeyball was the force behind the first great women's team in the 1890s. The British Ladies Club drew large crowds for its exhibition games in London at a time when the capital was lagging behind the North and Midlands of England with regard to soccer.

YOUNG TALENT
In the 1970s, Dutch team Ajax's policy to develop its own young players bore fruit. The players, including the star Johann Cruyff, helped Ajax to three consecutive European Cup wins in the 1970s, and some of them helped the national team in two World Cups. Despite regularly selling its best players, the team returned to the forefront of European soccer in the mid-1990s.

The team Ajax was formed in Amsterdam in 1900.

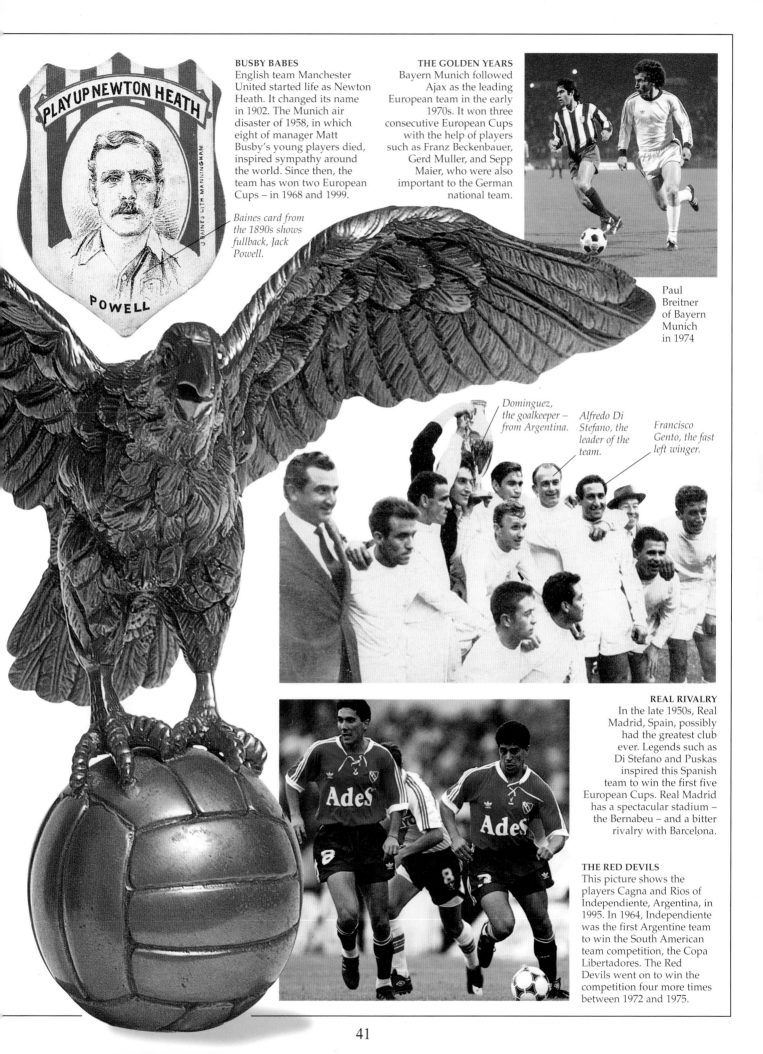

BUSBY BABES
English team Manchester United started life as Newton Heath. It changed its name in 1902. The Munich air disaster of 1958, in which eight of manager Matt Busby's young players died, inspired sympathy around the world. Since then, the team has won two European Cups – in 1968 and 1999.

Baines card from the 1890s shows fullback, Jack Powell.

PLAY UP NEWTON HEATH

POWELL

THE GOLDEN YEARS
Bayern Munich followed Ajax as the leading European team in the early 1970s. It won three consecutive European Cups with the help of players such as Franz Beckenbauer, Gerd Muller, and Sepp Maier, who were also important to the German national team.

Paul Breitner of Bayern Munich in 1974

Dominguez, the goalkeeper – from Argentina.

Alfredo Di Stefano, the leader of the team.

Francisco Gento, the fast left winger.

REAL RIVALRY
In the late 1950s, Real Madrid, Spain, possibly had the greatest club ever. Legends such as Di Stefano and Puskas inspired this Spanish team to win the first five European Cups. Real Madrid has a spectacular stadium – the Bernabeu – and a bitter rivalry with Barcelona.

THE RED DEVILS
This picture shows the players Cagna and Rios of Independiente, Argentina, in 1995. In 1964, Independiente was the first Argentine team to win the South American team competition, the Copa Libertadores. The Red Devils went on to win the competition four more times between 1972 and 1975.

The fans

GONE BANANAS
In England in the late 1980s, there was a craze for taking large inflatable objects to matches. Fans waved bananas, fish, and fried eggs in the crowd to show their support for their teams.

F̲OR ALL THE̲ talent displayed by the players on the field, it is the fans who have made soccer the biggest game in the world. From the last years of the 19th century, working people began to have enough free time to attend sports events. They created an atmosphere of excitement and expectation, and large crowds became an important part of a match. Today, soccer is the most widely watched sport in the world. Fans are more eager than ever to show their support for team and country in a range of noisy and colorful ways.

Manchester City, England, pennant

Preston North End, England, rosette

Holland scarf

PERFECT VIEW
In their desperation to see a game, fans are not always put off by the "sold out" signs. In the 19th century, before large-scale stands were built, trees provided a convenient spot from which to watch a popular match.

CLUB COLOURS
Colours are a vital part of the bond between a team and its supporters. Once, people made rosettes for big matches and displayed pennants. Now, fans often wear a scarf to show their loyalty.

Lazio, Italy, scarf

RARE COLLECTION
Fans have always collected objects bearing images of soccer. Today the items probably feature their favorite team but, in the past, designs were based on more general soccer scenes. Collecting autographs is also a popular hobby and offers a rare opportunity to meet star players.

Jack Rowley, forward

John Aston, full-back

Johnny Carey, full-back

Matt Busby, manager

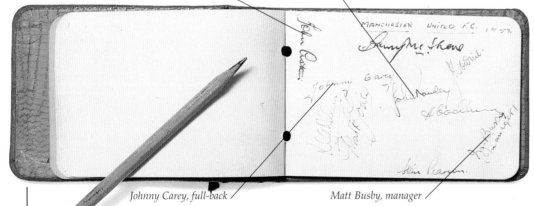

Child's money box

1950s autograph book containing signatures of famous figures of Manchester United, England.

Wooden pencil case

During the war, the sound of the bell warned people of an air raid.

Air-raid patrolman's rattle

Air-raid patrolman's bell

Rattles were originally used as bird scarers.

Top section moves around and around horizontally.

Adult's rattle

"Rattling" noise created at the handle

NOISY SUPPORT

Rattles were part of the atmosphere at games until the 1960s. When the horizontal section of the rattle is whirled around the "clicker" on the handle, it produces a loud rattling noise. Since the 1960s, organized chanting has become more common. Modern safety regulations restrict what items may be taken into the stadium, and rattles are no longer allowed.

Child's rattle

Child's rattle painted with a soccer scene

WAR CRY

Fans have taken bells and rattles to matches to express their support since before 1940. This bell and rattle were part of an air-raid patrolman's equipment in England World War II. In 1946, after the war, a Derby County fan took them to matches during Derby's run to the English FA Cup final.

WORLD BEATERS

Brazilian fans were famous for their noisy support long before the rest of the world discovered paints and drums. They produce a samba beat on their drums and blow their whistles. As the noise echoes around the stands, the fans dance to accompany the action, especially if their team is winning.

AFRICAN PAINTING

Face painting has become commonplace at major international matches, adding to the color and spectacle of the occasion. Here, two Zambian fans, painted to reflect the team's colours, enjoy an African Nations Cup match. Face painting is particularly popular with Dutch, Danish, and Japanese fans.

Game day

This is a scoreboard from an early 20th century French soccer game.

THE ATMOSPHERE of a big game, the sound of the crowd, and the closeness of the players combine to make going to a live soccer game quite addictive. Even though soccer is now widely shown on television, millions of fans still go to the game. Many supporters, like players, are extremely superstitious and follow the same routine every time they attend a game. The fans and the noisy support they give their team are essential to the game of soccer. It is vital that teams continue to improve comfort and safety for their fans, so that they keep on coming back.

ALL DRESSED UP
This photo shows fans of West Ham, England, preparing to travel to the 1923 FA Cup final, the first to be held at Wembley. Many more than the official attendance of 123,000 crammed into the stadium. Notice the neat and formal appearance of the supporters.

In the 1988 European Championship final, Holland beat the Soviet Union 2-0.

Holograms and complicated designs are now used to deter ticket forgeries.

TICKETS PLEASE
Tickets are essential in controlling access to games. Years ago, this was necessary only at cup finals and World Cup matches. Tickets were issued for general areas in the stadium. Now that terraces, areas for standing spectators, are being phased out in favor of seating, each match ticket corresponds to a particular seat.

READING MATTER
The earliest programs were simple one-sheet items, giving only team lineups. As soccer became more popular, further elements were added, such as a message from the manager and background information on the opposition. Glossy, full-color brochures, largely paid for by advertising, are produced for tournaments such as the European Championships.

LET ME ENTERTAIN YOU
To make going to a game even more enjoyable, particularly for a family audience, teams and governing bodies provide extra entertainment before kick-off and at halftime. In the past, this may have taken the form of a brass band, but modern crowds expect something more elaborate. The opening ceremony at France '98 featured giant inflatable soccer balls.

A FAMILY AFFAIR

In the US, a trip to a sporting event is usually a family day out, and the stadiums have good facilities for everybody. There is a lot of razzmatazz at the Major League Soccer games. Cheerleaders and music keep the crowds well entertained. This is game day at the Kansas City Wizards' stadium.

1903 FA official's patch

Official patch from 1905

The patches are made of cloth and decorated with gold brocade.

FA patch from 1898

The English three lions motif

BACKSTAGE PASS

Away from the mass of spectators, there are certain areas of the stadium, such as the boardroom, where access is strictly controlled. These patches, from 1898–1905, would have been sewn on blazers and worn by Football Association officials. These days, executive boxes have become a feature of many stadiums.

Patch worn at 1899 England v. Scotland International

CROWD CONTROL

Police attend soccer matches to ensure the safety of everybody at the game. Police, like these Italian officers at a Juventus game, may need to take a hard line with unruly fans, and sometimes use horses or dogs to help them control large crowds. They may also control traffic and escort supporters to and from the game.

COMING HOME

This drawing comes from a postcard from the early 20th century. The caption on the card says, "Our team's lost by – goals to – ." Space is left on the card for fans to fill in the score. Somehow, the depression of defeat is always replaced by excitement and high hopes when the next game comes around.

The stadium

AS CROWDS GREW EVER larger in the late 19th century, soccer teams realized that they would have to build permanent venues in which to hold their games. Stadiums became a necessity. They provided fans with shelter and a decent view of the game. They also created an atmosphere that added greatly to the game-day experience. A series of stadium disasters over the years, in places such as Scotland, Peru, and Russia, finally led to widespread belief that standing areas should be replaced by stands with seats, for the safety of spectators.

SHEFFIELD WEDNESDAY F.C.

THEN THERE WAS LIGHT...
Floodlights were first used in 1878, but they didn't become standard at professional games until the 1950s. The most common form of stadium lighting was on tall pylons in the corners of the stadium. Today, lights are often placed in rows along the stand roof.

CROWD SAFETY
On April 15, 1989, the FA Cup semifinal in Hillsborough, Sheffield, was the scene of the worst disaster in English soccer history. Ninety-six Liverpool fans died as a result of a crowd crush. The report into the tragedy began a major leap forward in stadium safety, to prevent a similar disaster from ever happening again.

WORLD CUP WONDER
The Maracana Stadium in Rio de Janeiro, Brazil, is named after a river that runs nearby. It was built for the 1950 World Cup. It is a huge concrete oval and has remained a source of wonder despite problems with its decaying structure. All the teams in Rio de Janeiro have their own grounds, but use the Maracana for big games. With its 120,000 capacity, it is one of the biggest stadiums in the world.

Lights along the top of the roof

STANDING TALLER
Barcelona, Spain, moved from Les Corts Stadium to the spectacular Nou Camp in 1957. Improvements for the 1982 World Cup and 1992 Olympics have increased the staggering height of the stands. The Nou Camp was paid for by the team's members.

PATH TO THE FIELD
The tunnel is more than just a route to the field. It is the place where players psych themselves up for the game and give in to their superstitions. Many insist on taking the same place in the line every time. Others put on their shirts only at the last moment.

The roof "hangs" from this crossbar.

The pylon is integral to the structure of the stand.

KEEPING UP TO DATE
Modern stands are designed using computer models to ensure that everybody has a good view. The space between seats is a difficult issue. More space means greater comfort, but it reduces the capacity of the stand. Designs, such as faces, are often picked out in the seats.

FANS ON THEIR FEET
Before all-seat stadiums were introduced, fans stood packed together on terraces. Far more fans could get in to watch a game and it is how the majority of people have watched games for much of soccer's history. Children were often passed over the heads of the crowd to the front to give them a better view.

STATE OF THE ART
The Stade de France is in St. Denis, north of Paris. It was built for the 1998 World Cup, and 80,000 spectators watched the opening game there between Brazil and Scotland. The stadium was widely praised for its dramatic design. The roof, enclosing the field in a continuous curve, creates an amphitheater effect, which has always been popular in European and South American stadiums.

Several tiers of seats

Field level openings for emergency vehicles

Revolving billboards around the field

The World Cup

THE SOCCER WORLD CUP is one of the greatest sports events of our time. The first World Cup was held in Uruguay in 1930, 26 years after FIFA first discussed the idea. In the early days, some teams were unable to travel to the host country, but by the 1950s, long-distance travel was becoming much easier and quicker. As the tournament became more accessible, it grew in popularity. The 1950 World Cup final at Maracana Stadium in Rio de Janeiro was attended by 200,000 people. In 1958, Brazilian teenager Pele became the first global soccer superstar. Since then, interest in the World Cup has boomed.

MANY MASCOTS
Every World Cup since 1966 has had a mascot. They appear as life-size figures at matches and scaled-down promotional or commercial images. This is Pique, from Mexico '86.

WORLD FIRST
Uruguay offered to pay travel and accommodation expenses to the 13 visiting teams at the first World Cup. Only four European teams made the long journey, joining the seven South American teams.

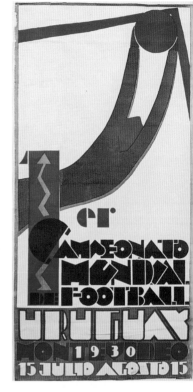

1954 – Switzerland. West Germany beat Hungary 3–2 in one of the great upsets in World Cup history.

1958 – Sweden. Brazil beat Sweden 5–2. Brazil is the only team to have played in every Finals tournament.

1950 – Brazil. Uruguay beat Brazil 2–1, in the first tournament after World War II.

1962 – Chile. Brazil beat Czechoslovakia 3–1, with Garrincha taking center stage after Pele was injured.

1938 – France. Italy beat Hungary 4–2, inspired by its star inside-forward, Meazza.

1966 – England. West Germany lost 2–4 to England in extra time, with Geoff Hurst scoring the first hat trick in a final.

1934 – Italy. Czechoslovakia lost 1–2 to Italy. Uruguay did not defend its crown, the only time this has happened.

1970 – Mexico. Brazil beat Italy 4–1 and were one of the greatest teams of all time.

1930 – Uruguay. Beating Argentina 4–2, Uruguay was the first of many host countries to win the Cup.

1974 – West Germany. Holland was beaten 2–1 by West Germany, which came back from being a goal behind.

VARIOUS VENUES
Competition to stage the World Cup Finals is always fierce because it brings visitors and publicity to the host country. The 2002 Finals, in Japan and South Korea, were the first shared tournament. Brazil beat Germany 2–0 in the final.

Argentina '78 is remembered for the tickertape in the River Plate Stadium.

Mexico was the first country to host two Finals.

The Italia '90 mascot was called Ciao.

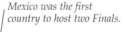

1978 – Argentina. Holland lost 1–3 to Argentina, leaving the Dutch as the best team never to have won the World Cup.

1982 – Spain. Italy beat West Germany 3–1, its striker Paolo Rossi finishing as leading scorer.

1986 – Mexico. Argentina beat West Germany 3–2, in a tournament dominated by Diego Maradona.

1990 – Italy. West Germany beat Argentina 1–0 in a defensive, bad-tempered final.

1998 – France. Brazil was beaten 3–0 by France in an amazingly one-sided match.

1994 – US. Brazil beat Italy 3–2 on penalties after a 0–0 draw and became the only team to have won four World Cups.

In 1994, American fans turned out in force to watch the matches.

The fans at Italia '90 provided more drama than some of the matches.

The figure is a winged seraphim.

Sweden, the host team, made it to the final in 1958 but was overpowered by the Brazilian superteam

The World Championship in Football 1958
Sweden 8–29 · 6

STOCKHOLM

GOTEBORG

HALSINGBORG
MALMÖ

Coupe Jules Rimet

READ ALL ABOUT IT
Programs for the World Cup are different from the team variety, in that they usually cover the whole tournament rather than a specific match. They contain information about the competing teams and are printed in several languages. These programs are from Sweden '58, England '66, Spain '82, Italy '90, and US '94.

WANDERING TROPHY
The first World Cup trophy was designed by a French sculptor, Abel Lafleur. Originally named "Victory," it was later named in honor of the president of FIFA, Jules Rimet. The trophy was stolen before the 1966 tournament in England and was found in a park by a dog called Pickles. Brazil was presented with the trophy to keep in 1970, but in 1983, it was stolen again and has not been seen since.

The trophy is made of solid gold.

The engraving on the trophy is in French.

COUPE DU MONDE
DE
FOOTBALL
ASSOCIATION
—
COUPE
JULES RIMET

Jules Rimet trophy

Didi

Pele was 17 in 1958.

Garrincha

THE BEAUTIFUL GAME
The 1958 final saw Brazil emerge as one of the World Cup's greatest teams. Its forward lineup was among the strongest in the game's history. Garrincha, Didi, Vava, Pele, and Zagalo drove the team to victory. Mario Zagalo later became the national team manager and was in charge when Brazil won again in 1970 and 1994.

Vava played at center-forward.

Zagalo, the left-winger scored the fourth goal in the final.

Continued on next page

WE MUST HAVE THE WORLD CUP
This was the poster for the 1962 Finals in Chile. A series of earthquakes marred the days before the tournament, but the hosts were determined. President of the Chilean FA, Carlos Dittborn, said, "We have nothing. That is why we must have the World Cup." Chile overcame the doubts of some European teams by staging a successful event. There was more trouble on the field than off it, particularly in the "Battle of Santiago" between Italy and Chile. Italy finished the game with nine men.

Globe forms the top of the trophy

World Cup Willie inspired a World Cup theme song by Lonnie Donnegan.

The Union Jack flag represents Great Britain, not just England.

Designed by Italian Silvio Gazzaniga, the trophy is made of solid 18-carat gold.

The real trophy is 20 in (50.8 cm) high and weighs 20 lbs (9 kg).

World Cup Willie was a lion, inspired by the three lions on the England uniform.

Replica of the World Cup trophy

MASCOTS FOR MONEY
World Cup Willie was the first World Cup mascot. Designed for the 1966 tournament in England, he represented the increase in commercialism. Since then tournament mascots, such as Ciao of Italy '90 and Footix of France '98, have appeared on official posters and been sold in many forms.

NEW LOOK CUP
The present World Cup trophy was made for the 1974 Finals in West Germany. Having won for the third time in 1970, Brazil had been allowed to keep the Jules Rimet trophy for good. The new trophy was commissioned by FIFA, despite an offer from Brazil to provide a trophy named after FIFA president, Sir Stanley Rous.

Argentina '78

Junio 1978
Buenos Aires
Córdoba
Mar del Plata
Mendoza
Rosario

THINKING POSITIVE
In 1978, host Argentina inspired its passionate fans with its positive attitude. The star of its winning team was Mario Kempes, who played team soccer in Europe.

Enter
GATE SEC ROW SEAT
F   222   11   4

Tuesday, June 28, 1994
R.F.K. Stadium
12:30 pm Kickoff

XV FIFA
World Cup

**GAME
30**

ITA vs MEX

$37.50   Category 2
WILLIAM SMART
Washington, D.C.

WorldCup USA 94

© 1991 WC'94 TM

oo ooo oo o o o o o

SEE REVERSE SIDE FOR TERMS AND CONDITIONS

ENTHUSIASTIC AMERICA
Despite having no strong tradition of professional soccer, the US hosted a successful World Cup Finals in 1994. Large and enthusiastic crowds attended all the games. This is a ticket for the game between Italy and Mexico, played at the former RFK Stadium, now the Jack Kent Cooke Stadium, home of American football team the Washington Redskins.

Spanish Football Federation crest

Information pack for Spain 1982

A pack of cards illustrating the stadiums

HARD WORK FOR HOSTS
A country bids to hold the World Cup several years in advance. It tries to convince FIFA that it will be able to stage a successful tournament. It has to produce information about all aspects of the tournament, including the stadiums, transportation networks, accommodations, and media facilities.

Fabien Barthez, France

The balls are brightly colored for the benefit of TV audiences.

Each ball contains a slip of paper with a team written on it.

Ronaldo, Brazil

Lilian Thuram, France

WHO PLAYS WHO?
Plastic balls like these are used to make the draw for the World Cup Finals. It is a fair way to decide who plays who. The number of competing teams has steadily increased from 13 in 1930 to 32 in 2002. The present system ensures that every team gets to play three games in the first round. Then, for the rest of the tournament, games are played on an elimination basis, until only two remain for the grand final.

2002
World Cup Japan

IN THE BAG
This bag is a promotional item for the 2002 World Cup, staged jointly by Japan and South Korea. It was the first shared tournament and the first one held in Asia. Demand is sure to increase for smaller countries to benefit from this arrangement.

FRANCE IN ACTION
Brazil was expected to retain its title in 1998, but doubts surrounding Ronaldo's fitness to play seemed to distract the team in the final. The goalkeeper Fabien Barthez was one of many members in the victorious French team who enhanced his reputation with a brilliant performance throughout the tournament.

Cups and trophies

THE MOMENT WHEN a team captain is presented with a trophy and holds it up to the fans is the crowning glory of any campaign. Cups and trophies are the marks of success, and the managers of many modern teams know that, if they are to hold on to their job, their team has to win a competition. For clubs like Real Madrid in Spain, Benfica in Portugal, and Bayern Munich in Germany, finishing as runners-up is considered a failure. The desire to make money has led to the creation, in recent years, of many new competitions, some of which do not have the same prestige as older tournaments such as the European Cup and the Copa America.

OLYMPIC SOCCER
This patch is from the 1956 Olympic Games. The Olympics featured demonstration soccer games from 1896. The first official Olympic tournament was in 1908.

TEAM TALK
The European Cup was originally for the champions of each country's league. Now some lower placed teams compete. The competition was first held in 1956. At the 1985 final at the Heysel Stadium in Brussels, Belgium, 39 people died. A safety wall collapsed as fans of Juventus, Italy, and Liverpool, England, fought each other.

Program for the 1985 European Cup final

Corner flags used as decoration

The gold-plated Women's World Cup trophy has a soccer ball at the top.

Holding the trophy aloft is a proud moment.

FULL HOUSE
In the 1999 Women's World Cup in the US, teams played in front of capacity crowds. The final was held in the Rose Bowl in Passadena, California. Here, US player Cindy Parlow rides a tackle in the final against China. The US won, to secure its second World Cup victory.

EARLY CUP
This decorative, silver-plated trophy from the 1870s is an example of an early soccer cup. After the FA Cup was started in 1872, local tournaments for small teams began to be set up all over England and Scotland along the same lines.

WOMEN'S WORLD CUP
The first Women's World Cup took place in China in 1991. The final was held in Guangzhou, where the US beat Norway 2–1. The tournament went from strength to strength and the next two events, in 1995 and 1999, drew large crowds. This is the trophy awarded to the US in 1999.

PLAYER'S CIGARETTES

ASSOCIATION CUP WINNERS
THE OLD CUP

PLAYER'S CIGARETTES

ASSOCIATION CUP W
THE PRESENT CUP

LITTLE TIN IDOLS
The first FA Cup, on the left, was known as the Little Tin Idol. It was stolen from a shop display in 1895 and was never recovered. The present FA Cup, on the right, was made in Bradford, England, in 1911.

The silver UEFA trophy is decorated with a design of men playing soccer.

Names of previous winners engraved around the base

FROM STRENGTH TO STRENGTH
The African Nations Cup has been held every two years since 1957. It has grown from humble beginnings, and as many as 16 teams now take part. Egyptian striker Hassan Hossam is pictured here after his team's 1998 triumph over the defending champions, South Africa. This was Egypt's fourth African Nations title.

COPA AMERICA CUP
First held in 1910, the Copa America is the oldest major international competition. It was originally played only by South American countries, but in recent years, Mexico and the US have also taken part. Uruguay won the first official Copa America in 1917 and, along with Argentina, has been the most successful team over the years. Brazil has not always played its strongest team. Since 1987, the tournament has been held every two years.

SECOND BEST
The UEFA (Union of European Football Associations) Cup was originally known as the Inter City Fairs Cup. The first competition was played over three years, beginning in 1955. Barcelona beat London 8–2 in the two-legged final. When the European Cup Winner's Cup was abolished in 1999, only two European team competitions remained. The strongest sides qualify for the European Cup, and the next best play in the UEFA Cup.

The Copa America was conceived by Chile, Uruguay, Brazil, and Argentina

Playing the game

GENERATIONS OF children have had their first contact with soccer through toys such as Fussball, card games, and Subbuteo. The popularity of soccer means that, as with other merchandise, there is money to be made from developing new products with a soccer theme. This drives manufacturers and inventors to come up with a vast range of games based on soccer, far more than on any other sport. The simplicity of the toys from the past, shown here, contrasts sharply with the speed and excitement of modern computer games. Today, children and adults can experience virtual soccer games and act out the roles of their favorite players and teams on Playstations and in computer games.

Two lead "kicking" figures from the early 20th century

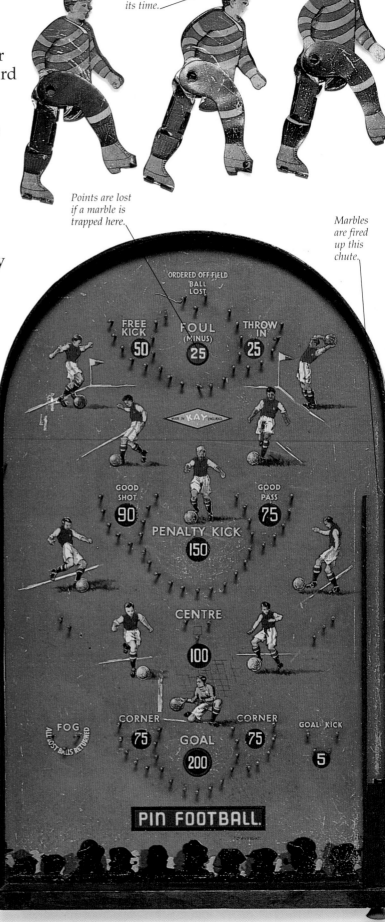

This game was advanced for its time.

Points are lost if a marble is trapped here.

Marbles are fired up this chute.

PIN FOOTBALL.

BALL ROLLING
This handheld toy was made in the early 20th century. It involves rolling the ball bearing into one of the small holes.

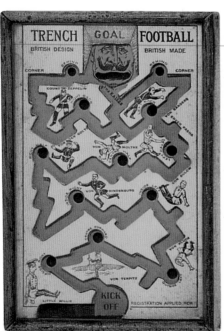

IN THE TRENCHES
Trench Soccer was produced for British soldiers fighting in World War I. The player must move a ball bearing safely past the German generals to score.

SOCCER MATCHBOX
This is the world's smallest soccer game, probably made in Japan in the 1930s for small children. When the matchbox is opened, a spring is released and the players leap up.

PINBALL
In this bagatelle game from the 1950s, players shoot marbles around the board using a spring in the bottom-right-hand corner. Points are scored or lost according to where the marbles stop.

54

Ball for the Kick game

Downward pressure on one leg causes the other leg to kick.

The cards feature different positions and parts of the game.

KICK FIGURES

These figures come from a tabletop game called Kick, made in about 1900. A green cloth field, and goals with nets are included. Players make the mechanical soccer players kick by pressing them down on the table. They are moved around by hand – a feature also used in more modern soccer toys.

Combination of red and white is a classic football strip

Key fits into the ball to wind it up

SNAP!

This rare pack of snap cards from the early 20th century features soccer characters. In snap, players aim to collect all the cards. They turn over cards until two identical ones turn up together. The first player to shout "Snap!" takes the pile.

CLOCKWORK PLAYER

This tin-plate clockwork toy was made in Germany in the early 1950s. When wound up with a key, the figure moves forward, as if dribbling the ball. The shirt, with its loosely laced neck, is typical of the style of soccer clothes worn in Europe at that time.

CHAMPIONS!

This game, called Championship Soccer, was made in 1983. It uses two of the classic components of many board games – dice and cards – to govern the movement of the ball around the field. A scoreboard and clock are also included.

QUICK CHANGE

These wooden blocks, with a different picture on each side, can be jumbled up to make a character. The shinpads and ball reflect the style of the time when the toy was made – 1895.

Memorabilia

SOCCER appeals to all parts of the community, regardless of age or sex. The game can therefore be used to promote a wide range of items. Soccer-related advertising and product promotion is not a new phenomenon. In fact, companies were already latching on to the game's popularity in the early part of the 20th century. An understated style and original artwork predominated until the 1950s. This has been largely replaced today by mass-produced items, heavily reliant on star players and wealthy clubs.

1910 silver Vesta (match holder) advertising the mustard maker Colman's

Bank Top White Star

Welsh national team

Wednesday, now Sheffield Wednesday

Scottish club, Hearts

Chadderton, a nonleague team

BAINES CARDS
These cards, produced in the late 19th and early 20th century, were the forerunners of sticker albums and other collectibles. They featured soccer and rugby league teams at professional and amateur level and had advertisements on the reverse side.

SPORTS CAN
By the 1930s, original artwork on a sports theme was often used as a decoration for everyday household items. This can features soccer on the lid and other sports, including cricket and hockey, around the outside.

Covered stands are rare in southern Europe.

FIFA logo for Italia '90

SOUVENIRS
Mementoes of the World Cup Finals do not stop at programs and tickets. There is great demand around the world for anything tied to the tournament, such as these erasers from Italia '90.

SOCCER FAN
This is a Spanish woman's fan from the mid 20th century, printed in Barcelona. It has a soccer image on one side and carries a promotional message on the reverse. Many commercial objects of this period were designed to be artistic as well as functional.

POSTER PAINTING
In this advertising card of the 1920s, an Italian drinks company has illustrated its product in a soccer scene, instead of putting a soccer image on the actual bottle.

VERMOUTH JACCOBINO

HEALTHY KICK
There is no magic ingredient in this drink, but the images would have appealed to soccer fans. The manufacturers knew that any association with soccer would improve sales.

This label comes from a fruity soft drink. It was marketed as an ideal refreshment for half-time.

This label implies that the drink will promote the strength that a soccer player enjoys.

FOOTBALL CUP SPECIAL QUALITY

Class B17 locomotive

Banks Johnstone Jennings England Best

TEAM TRAIN
In the early 1980s, the Hornby toy company of Liverpool, England, produced a series of these scale models of the London North Eastern Railway's locomotives, named after soccer teams. This one is called the *Manchester United*. Real trains are also sometimes named after teams.

Name plate

The kicking leg is the second hand.

GASOLINE HEADS
The Cleveland Petrol company produced these miniatures of British international players in 1971. The set was given away free with gasoline sales.

Pocket watch

Watch

Alarm clock

FULL TIME
This group includes a Swiss pocket watch made in Geneva around 1910, a British watch from the 1950s, and a more modern 1970s alarm clock. Design, materials, and, therefore, cost were dictated by whether the object was aimed at children or adults.

Chain

CHAIN MEDALS
Soccer items are often turned into jewelry and other personal effects. Four silver medals, struck in the 1920s, are attached to this chain. The silver locket and compass are from the 1880s.

Locket

Compass

More medals could be added to the chain.

OLYMPIC CLOCK
This German wooden clock may well have been made to commemorate the 1936 Berlin Olympics, where the soccer tournament was won by Italy, when they beat Austria 2–1 in the final. The figures at the top of the clock move on the hour.

The figure is the same on both halves.

SOAP ON A ROPE
The Avon company produced this soap soccer ball to mark the 1966 World Cup Finals in England.

STRING ALONG
Made in the 1880s, this copper string holder prevents string from getting tangled. The string is pulled through a hole in the top.

CHOCOLATE
Melted chocolate would have been poured into this early 20th century brass mold and left to cool and set, producing a miniature chocolate soccer player with a ball at his feet. This item was made to appeal mainly to children, and the general soccer theme would have been enough to make it popular.

The business of soccer

SOCCER IS BIG BUSINESS – fans attend games in large numbers, team products sell worldwide, and top players and managers earn incredibly large salaries. The people who started professionalism in the 1880s realized the financial possibilities of soccer, but for many decades the game carried on at much the same level. It provided inexpensive entertainment to the paying public and offered a decent living to players and managers. All that has changed now, as club owners and star players stretch soccer's money-making potential to the limit.

Gullit, pictured here in a preseason game, occasionally played for the teams he was managing as player-manager.

The emblem of the sponsoring local brewery

Even shinpads, worn under the socks, are marked with the name of the manufacturer.

BILLY'S BRIBE

This shirt was worn by Welshman Billy Meredith, the greatest player of his era. As a player for Manchester City, England, he was barred from playing for a year in 1905. He allegedly tried to bribe the Aston Villa captain, offering him £10 ($50) to lose an important game. This was the first major scandal of British soccer.

GETTING SHIRTY

Replica shirts are a major source of income for professional teams like England's Manchester United and Spain's Real Madrid. Three or four designs are now available at one time, and new ones are brought out at regular intervals. Clubs produce hundreds of different products – from calenders to baby clothes; from candy to bicycles. These can be sold to fans all over the world, reducing the team's reliance on gate receipts.

MANAGEMENT STRESS

Managers are subjected to great stress in the modern game and have to accept that their every decision will be examined by the media. In most of the major leagues, the length of time allowed for a manager to produce a winning team can be measured in months rather than years. In 1999, Ruud Gullit was forced out of his job as manager of England's Newcastle United after just a few unsuccessful months.

SHIRT AD

In the 1970s, businesses began to pay for the right to advertise on team uniforms. Within a few years, even nonleague teams had some income from this source. Pictured here are players from Real Madrid, Spain, and Inter Milan, Italy, sporting their sponsor's logos.

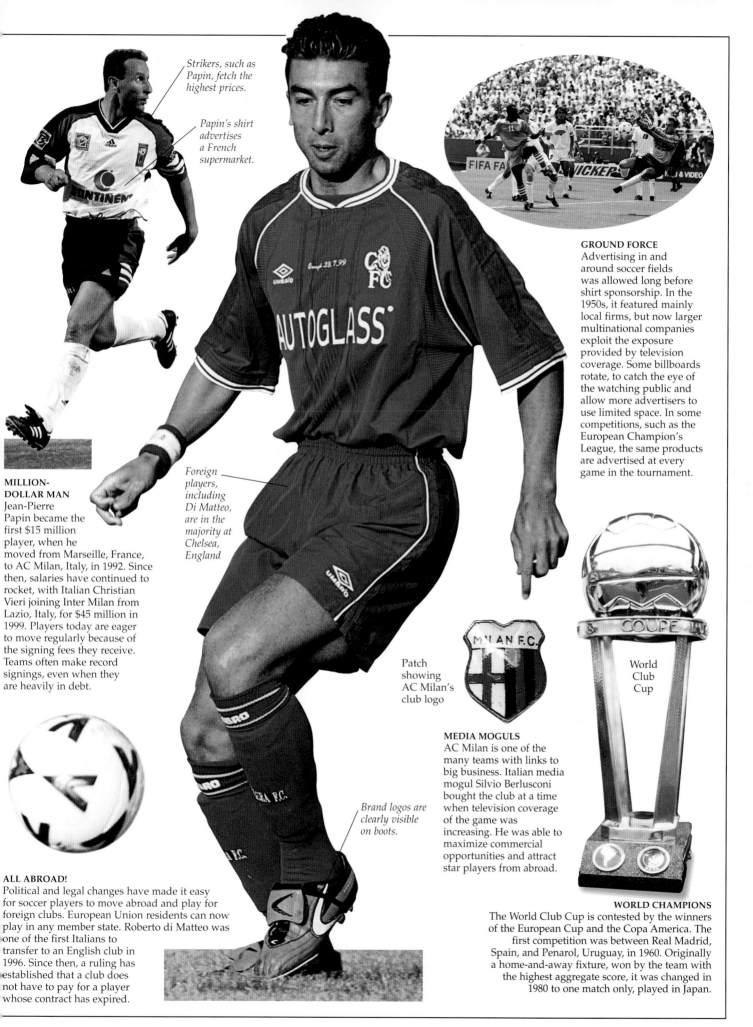

Strikers, such as Papin, fetch the highest prices.

Papin's shirt advertises a French supermarket.

GROUND FORCE
Advertising in and around soccer fields was allowed long before shirt sponsorship. In the 1950s, it featured mainly local firms, but now larger multinational companies exploit the exposure provided by television coverage. Some billboards rotate, to catch the eye of the watching public and allow more advertisers to use limited space. In some competitions, such as the European Champion's League, the same products are advertised at every game in the tournament.

MILLION-DOLLAR MAN
Jean-Pierre Papin became the first $15 million player, when he moved from Marseille, France, to AC Milan, Italy, in 1992. Since then, salaries have continued to rocket, with Italian Christian Vieri joining Inter Milan from Lazio, Italy, for $45 million in 1999. Players today are eager to move regularly because of the signing fees they receive. Teams often make record signings, even when they are heavily in debt.

Foreign players, including Di Matteo, are in the majority at Chelsea, England

Patch showing AC Milan's club logo

World Club Cup

MEDIA MOGULS
AC Milan is one of the many teams with links to big business. Italian media mogul Silvio Berlusconi bought the club at a time when television coverage of the game was increasing. He was able to maximize commercial opportunities and attract star players from abroad.

Brand logos are clearly visible on boots.

ALL ABROAD!
Political and legal changes have made it easy for soccer players to move abroad and play for foreign clubs. European Union residents can now play in any member state. Roberto di Matteo was one of the first Italians to transfer to an English club in 1996. Since then, a ruling has established that a club does not have to pay for a player whose contract has expired.

WORLD CHAMPIONS
The World Club Cup is contested by the winners of the European Cup and the Copa America. The first competition was between Real Madrid, Spain, and Penarol, Uruguay, in 1960. Originally a home-and-away fixture, won by the team with the highest aggregate score, it was changed in 1980 to one match only, played in Japan.

Did you know?

AMAZING FACTS

A soft-boiled egg

⚽ On average, each player in a game has the ball for only three minutes, the time it takes to soft-boil an egg.

⚽ In 1965, substitutes were allowed in soccer for the first time, but only when a player was injured. Substitutes were first used in the World Cup in 1970.

⚽ Luis Chilavert, goalkeeper for Paraguay, rushed out of his goal and scored for his team in a game against Argentina in 1998. The final score was 1–1.

⚽ The first person to score from a penalty in a World Cup final was Johan Neeskens for Holland in 1974.

⚽ In the 1994 World Cup finals, Russia failed to qualify for the later stages even though they scored more goals in the first stage of the competition than any other team.

⚽ The referee for the 1930 World Cup final wore a shirt, tie, jacket and short pants.

⚽ Johann Cruyff's mother was a cleaning woman for the Dutch soccer team Ajax. When she persuaded them to give her 10-year-old son a trial, they signed him as a youth player. He went on to become an international soccer star.

⚽ The goal net did not become compulsory until 1892. The crossbar was introduced in 1875.

⚽ The first time teams used numbered shirts in an FA Cup final was in 1933. Everton wore numbers one to 11, and Manchester City wore numbers 12 to 22.

⚽ Eight of the players who won the World Cup for Brazil in 1958 were on the team that retained the World Cup in 1962.

⚽ Pele scored 1,283 goals in his senior career.

⚽ Half of the world's registered soccer players are from Asia. Hide Nakata is one of the first Japanese players to make a career outside his country.

Hide Nakata

⚽ Only seven different countries have been World Cup champions, although there have been 17 finals.

⚽ The FA Cup is the oldest competition in soccer. The highest-scoring FA Cup victory was on October 15, 1887, when Preston North End beat Hyde United 26–0 in the first round of the competition. The score was 12–0 at halftime and 25–0 at 90 minutes. The final goal was scored in the five minutes of extra time added by the referee.

Tony Adams of Arsenal with the FA Cup

⚽ After Brazil beat Italy 4–1 in the 1970 World Cup final, reporters pursued Pele into the locker room and interviewed him while he took a shower!

⚽ Uruguay, host nation of the first World Cup in 1930, offered to pay travel expenses for every team.

⚽ The first international soccer game played by a side with 12 players was in 1952, between France and Northern Ireland. One of the French players was injured and substituted, but after treatment he continued playing, and no one noticed until halftime.

⚽ Two pairs of brothers, John and Mel Charles and Len and Ivor Allchurch, played on the Welsh team that beat Northern Ireland 3–2 in 1955. John Charles scored a hat trick.

QUESTIONS AND ANSWERS

Q How many women play soccer in the United States?

A Soccer is the most popular women's sport in the United States, with around eight million players. The women's national team won their first World Cup in 1991 and won it again in 1999. They were Olympic champions in 1996, lost narrowly in 2000, then won gold by defeating Brazil 2–1 in 2004.

Q Why was the first World Cup held in Uruguay?

A Uruguay hosted the first World Cup in 1930, because they were Olympic champions at the time.

Q Were old soccer balls heavier than those used today?

A Watching old footage of soccer games, people often make the mistake of thinking that soccer balls used to be heavier. In fact, they were virtually the same weight, but today's balls have a special coating that stops the leather from absorbing moisture. Before this development, soccer balls could absorb water freely, and on wet days the ball could double in weight, often making it as heavy as 2.2 lb (1 kg).

Mia Hamm

Leather soccer ball

Q When were floodlights first used in a soccer game?

A The first recorded use of floodlights was at Bramall Lane, Sheffield, England in 1878. The lamps were placed on wooden gantries and were powered by generators.

Q Why were women banned from playing on the grounds of FA clubs in 1921?

A On December 26, 1920, more than 53,000 spectators packed into Everton's Goodison Park to watch Dick Kerr Ladies play St. Helens Ladies. The FA, worried that the women's game was becoming more popular than the men's game, banned women from playing on FA club grounds. The ban was not lifted until 1970.

Q Which country was the first to be knocked out of a World Cup in a penalty shoot-out?

A Penalty shoot-outs were introduced into the World Cup finals in 1982, and in the semifinals West Germany knocked out France in a penalty shoot-out.

Q Who plays soccer in the Olympic Games?

A The national women's football teams compete in the Olympics, but for men it is the national under-23 teams that take part.

Q Who was England's first black professional soccer player?

A Arthur Wharton, originally from the Gold Coast (now Ghana), played for Preston North End as an amateur in the 1880s. He then went on to play as a professional for Rotherham Town, Sheffield United, and Stockport County. He was also a gifted sprinter and could run 100 yards (91 m) in 10 seconds.

Q Why have there been three different FA Cup trophies?

A The first trophy was stolen while on display in a Birmingham, England, sports shop window after Aston Villa's 1895 victory, so a second trophy, a replica of the first, was made. When Manchester United won the FA Cup in 1909, they made a copy of this second trophy for one of their directors. As a result, the FA withdrew this trophy and made the third and current FA Cup trophy. Manufactured in 1911, it bears no resemblance to the original 1872 trophy.

Q What does the phrase "back to square one" have to do with soccer?

A When the BBC first broadcast soccer live on radio in 1927, the radio guide printed a diagram of the field, divided into numbered squares. When the ball was passed back to the goalkeeper, the commentators would say, "Back to square one."

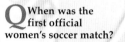

BBC radio microphone

Q When was the first official women's soccer match?

A Netty Honeyball, secretary of the British Ladies Football Club, organized the first women's soccer match in 1895.

Record Breakers

⚽ Brazil has won the World Cup five times, more than any other country.

⚽ The oldest football club in the world is Sheffield FC, formed in 1857. The founders wrote and used their own rules until 1878.

⚽ Lev Yashin (Russia) is the only goalkeeper who has been chosen as European Footballer of the Year.

⚽ In 1999, Manchester United became the first team to win the Treble of the Premier League, the FA Cup, and the European Champions League.

⚽ Real Madrid has won the European Champions League eight times, more than any other team.

⚽ In 1957, Stanley Matthews became the oldest man to play for England when he won his 84th international cap at the age of 42. He continued playing Division One football until he was 50 years old.

Stanley Matthews collector's card

7
S. MATTHEWS ENGLAND

Who's who?

SOCCER IS A GAME OF SPEED and skill, and there are many outstanding players. With international competitions like the FIFA World Cup, extensive media coverage, and a transfer system that allows players to sign for teams in other countries, players from all parts of the world can become household names. Referees can also build up a considerable reputation around the world. These pages contain some of the past and present players who are among the world's best but who have not been featured in the earlier pages of this book.

Italian referee Pierluigi Collina

GOALKEEPERS

• SEPP MAIER, WEST GERMANY, BORN 2/28/44
The pinnacle of Maier's distinguished career was in 1974, when he won the European Cup with Bayern Munich, followed by the World Cup with West Germany. He played with Bayern Munich for a total of 19 years.

• PETER SHILTON, ENGLAND, BORN 9/18/49
Renowned for his fitness and perfectionism, Shilton made his senior England debut when he was only 20 years old. Over the next 21 years he played for his country 125 times.

• PETER SCHMEICHEL, DENMARK, BORN 11/18/63
In 1991, Schmeichel moved to Manchester United, where he has won five league titles and two FA Cups. In his trademark "star" save, Schmeichel runs out, spreads his arms and legs wide, and jumps toward the striker.

• DINO ZOFF, ITALY, BORN 2/28/42
Tall and determined, Zoff was almost impossible to beat. He appeared 112 times for Italy between 1968 and 1983 and captained Italy when they won the World Cup in 1982. With Juventus, he won six Italian League titles and the UEFA Cup.

Dino Zoff

DEFENDERS

• FRANCO BARESI, ITALY, BORN 5/8/60
The best sweeper in the world for much of the 1980s and 1990s, Baresi would bring the ball forward and join in attacks. He retired in 1997, having played more than 600 times for club team AC Milan during his 20-year career.

Franco Baresi

• MARCEL DESAILLY, FRANCE, BORN 9/7/68
Born in Accra, Ghana, Desailly moved to France when he was a child. In 1993 and 1994, he won the Champions Cup twice, first with Marseille and then with AC Milan. Desailly played a vital role for the French national team when they won the World Cup in 1998 and the European Championship in 2000.

• PAUL BREITNER, WEST GERMANY, BORN 9/5/51
An adventurous, skilled left back with Bayern Munich, Breitner moved forward to midfield when he transfered to Real Madrid. He was relaxed and seemingly nerveless in big matches.

• ROBERTO CARLOS DA SILVA, BRAZIL, BORN 4/10/73
A player of great skill, with a reputation for taking ferocious free kicks, Roberto Carlos joined the Brazilian national team after the 1994 World Cup. A runner-up in 1998, he won the World Cup in 2002. He joined Real Madrid in 1996, helping them dominate the Spanish league in his first season and win the UEFA Champions League Final in his second.

• FERNANDO RUIZ HIERRO, SPAIN, BORN 3/23/68
A gifted central defender, Hierro's sure-footed tackling helped Real Madrid win the UEFA Champions League Finals in both 1998 and 2002.

• PAOLO MALDINI, ITALY, BORN 6/26/68
An attacking fullback and one of the best defenders in the world, Maldini has captained AC Milan and Italy, appearing for Italy more than 120 times.

Bobby Moore

• BOBBY MOORE, ENGLAND, BORN 4/12/41
A great defender and an excellent captain, Bobby Moore led England to victory in the 1966 World Cup. He played for England 108 times, missing only 10 matches between 1962 and 1972.

• OSCAR RUGGERI, ARGENTINA, BORN 1/26/62
Ruggeri was the heart of the Argentine defense in the 1980s and a World Cup winner in Mexico in 1986. He captained his national side and won a total of 89 caps.

MIDFIELDERS

• LUIS FILIPE MADEIRA CAEIRO FIGO, PORTUGAL, BORN 11/4/72
Figo was a European champion in the under-16 level in 1989, and a World Youth Cup winner in 1991. He won the Portuguese Cup with Sporting Clube in 1995, and then moved to Barcelona, where he led the team to the Spanish league title in 1998, before moving on to play for Real Madrid.

• PAUL GASCOIGNE, ENGLAND, BORN 5/27/67
An extremely gifted player who possessed excellent ball control and passing skills, Gascoigne's career was hampered by injuries. He was an important member of England's 1990 World Cup team.

• ALAIN GIRESSE, FRANCE, BORN 9/2/52
A skillful player with excellent technique, Giresse was at the heart of the French midfield at the 1982 World Cup finals and the 1984 European Championships.

• GHEORGHE HAGI, ROMANIA, BORN 2/5/65
Romania's greatest player of all time, Hagi was a youth international at 15 and a full international at 18. An outstanding midfield presence, he went on to play in Romania, Spain, Italy, and Turkey.

• FRANK RIJKAARD, HOLLAND, BORN 9/30/62
Rijkaard made his debut for Holland at the age of 19. A universally admired and versatile player, he played midfield for Milan and central defense for Holland. He moved around Europe, playing for clubs in Holland, Portugal, Spain, and Italy.

• VITOR FERREIRA BARBOSA (RIVALDO), BRAZIL, BORN 4/19/74
A fast, attacking midfielder, Rivaldo has skillful ball control and excellent passing skills. A great scorer, he can shoot with either foot, and is often successful with unorthodox overhead shots. He was a key player in the Brazilian national squad in the 1990s and was named FIFA World Player of the Year in 1999.

Gheorghe Hagi

• SOCRATES, BRAZIL, BORN 2/19/54
A player with tremendous balance and poise, Socrates made excellent passes, and scored terrific goals. He was a doctor before becoming a player, and returned to medicine once his soccer days were over.

• ZINEDINE ZIDANE, FRANCE, BORN 6/23/72
An outstandingly skillful player, Zidane was voted Young Player of the Year in 1992. He scored two goals in his national debut for France and was FIFA's World Player of the Year both in 1998 and in 2000. A creative and inspirational player, composed and confident on the field, he scored two of his country's three goals against Brazil in the 1998 World Cup final in Paris, becoming a French national hero.

Socrates

FORWARDS

• ROBERTO BAGGIO, ITALY, BORN 2/18/67
A world-class scorer, Baggio helped Juventus win the UEFA Cup in 1993 and the league title in 1995. He was both FIFA's World Player of the Year and European Footballer of the Year in 1993.

• GEORGE BEST, NORTHERN IRELAND, BORN 5/22/46
An amazingly gifted player, Best had excellent ball skills and balance. He was European Footballer of the Year in 1968. Many feel that he could have played at the highest level for a longer time if his success with his club team, Manchester United, had continued.

• KENNY DALGLISH, SCOTLAND, BORN 3/4/51
Probably Scotland's greatest player ever, Dalglish had excellent ball-control skills and was able to slice through a defense with his bold, accurate passes.

• THIERRY HENRY, FRANCE, BORN 8/17/77
A striker possessing terrific ball control, incredible pace, and clinical finishing, Henry was the top goal scorer for France when they won the World Cup in 1998.

• RAUL GONZALEZ BLANCO, SPAIN, BORN 6/27/77
An extremely skilled player with a knack for being in the right place at the right time, Raul scores stunning goals, both with his head and his feet.

• RONALDO LUIS NAZARIO, BRAZIL, BORN 9/22/76
Ronaldo scored his first goal for Brazil when he was only 16 years old. An exciting, inspirational striker, his speed and skill enable him to break through almost any defense. Ronaldo was FIFA's World Player of the Year in both 1996 and 1997.

George Best

• KARL-HEINZ RUMMENIGGE, WEST GERMANY, BORN 9/25/55
European Footballer of the Year in 1980 and 1981, Rummenigge was a formidable forward capable of cutting through a team's defense. Between 1976 and 1986, he appeared 95 times for West Germany, scoring 45 goals.

• CHRISTIAN VIERI, ITALY, BORN 7/12/73
A fast, decisive striker, Vieri ended his first season with Madrid in 1998 as the Spanish league's top scorer, with 24 goals. He scored five more for Italy in the 1998 World Cup finals.

Thierry Henry

Find out more

THERE ARE MANY WAYS to get more involved in the world of soccer. An important start is to find a team you want to support, and follow their performance. If you like to play yourself, you can join a team and take part in a local league. By visiting museums such as the National Soccer Hall of Fame, you will find out about managers, coaches, and scouts as well as players to help you build up a picture of the world of soccer. The more you learn, the more you will enjoy the soccer fever surrounding the big competitions, such as the World Cup finals.

REMEMBER THE GAME
Programs are full of information about the teams that are playing and they're also a great keepsake of an exciting event.

Bob Bishop was the Manchester United scout who discovered George Best, Sammy McIlroy, and many others in the 1960s and 1970s

USEFUL WEB SITES

- To find out about the Football Association: **www.thefa.com**
- For information on the World Cup: **www.fifa.com**
- To develop your soccer skills with great players: **http://news.bbc.co.uk/sportacademy/hi/sa/football/**
- Excited about soccer in the United States? Then visit the home of Major League Soccer—be sure to check out the youth programs: **www.mlsnet.com**
- For U.S. soccer scores, team information, photos, news, and tickets: **www.ussoccer.com**
- Want the latest scores plus up-to-the-minute headlines? Visit: **www.usatoday.com/sports/soccer/front.htm**
- For up-to-date soccer information and all scores: **news.bbc.co.uk/sport2/hi/football/default.stm**

SUPPORT YOUR TEAM
Decide which team you want to support and start following their results. If you can, go to some games and start your own collection of programs. Watching the games and reading the programs, you will soon become an expert on your team's players and management. You will also learn about soccer rules and will even have your own ideas on tactics and how the team should be run. If you get a chance to go to an international game, you will meet supporters from other parts of the world.

SOCCER SCOUTS
All big teams have scouts who travel around looking for new talent, whether it be established players that the club can "buy," or gifted youth players. Outstanding young players will be asked to participate in a trial, and if they are successful, may be invited to join the club's training academy. Here they will receive a general education as well as intensive soccer training. If all goes well they will work up through the youth and reserve teams to play in the club's first-string team.

Italian fans cheer for their team

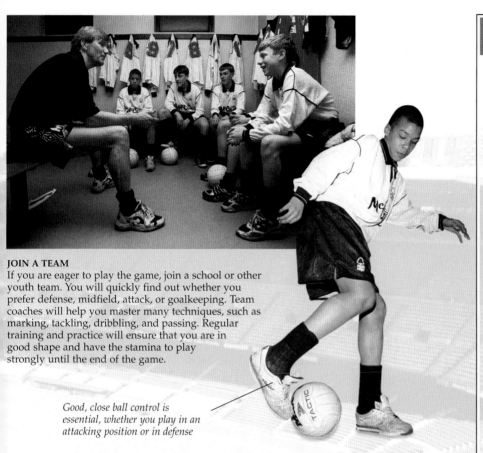

JOIN A TEAM

If you are eager to play the game, join a school or other youth team. You will quickly find out whether you prefer defense, midfield, attack, or goalkeeping. Team coaches will help you master many techniques, such as marking, tackling, dribbling, and passing. Regular training and practice will ensure that you are in good shape and have the stamina to play strongly until the end of the game.

Good, close ball control is essential, whether you play in an attacking position or in defense

THE 2006 FIFA WORLD CUP™

In the summer of 2006, the FIFA World Cup finals will take place in Germany. Thirty-two teams will compete in a total of 64 games, which will be played in 12 different cities around Germany, from Hamburg in the north to Munich in the south. Qualifying games were initiated in January 2004, and will continue around the world until 2006. Hundreds of thousands of fans will gather in Germany for the finals, and they will be a proving ground for German mass transit, accommodations, and police.

Places to visit

NATIONAL SOCCER HALL OF FAME AND MUSEUM, ONEONTA, NEW YORK

www.soccerhall.org

Established in 1979, the National Soccer Hall of Fame has housed an extensive archive of memorabilia associated with soccer in the United States for almost 20 years. The star of the museum is the Kicks Zone, a hands-on, feet-on interactive area that lets kids and adults actually kick and head balls and play unique computer games as well. Test your skills and your strategy with speed dribbles, a header cage, animated "Kick It" games, power shots, the Wall, and three-on-three challenges. Computer kiosks throughout the museum let visitors test their knowledge of soccer skills and trivia. Make sure to wear your sneakers!

THE SOCCER HALL OF FAME AND MUSEUM, VAUGHN, ONTARIO, CANADA

(905) 264-9390

The museum displays many soccer treasures and a wall of inductees to the hall of fame.

D.C. UNITED
MAJOR LEAGUE SOCCER
RFK STADIUM
WASHINGTON, D.C.

(202) 432-SEAT (7328)

You can watch pro soccer played by D.C. United, or by any of the other major-league teams in the country. Along with D.C. United, the Eastern Conference teams include the Chicago Fire, Columbus Crew, Metrostars, and New England Revolution; in the Western Conference, look for the Colorado Rapids, Dallas Burn, Kansas City Wizards, Los Angeles Galaxy, and San Jose Earthquakes. Visit www.mlsnet.com/MLS/teams/ to get the schedule for your team.

In all FIFA competitions, a Fair Play Trophy is awarded to the team with the best behavior

FIFA fair play logo, introduced in 1993

Glossary

AFRICAN NATIONS CUP First won in 1957; African national teams compete for the trophy every two years

AGENT The person who acts on behalf of a player in the arrangement of a transfer or a new contract

ASSISTANT REFEREES Formerly known as linesmen, one of these officials covers each half of the field, signaling offsides, throw-ins, fouls, and substitutions

BOOK The referee books players when they have committed an offense by showing them a yellow card and writing their names in his black book. Players are ejected if they receive two yellow cards in one game.

CAP Originally a hat awarded to those playing in an international match; caps now serve as a symbolic tally of a player's international appearances

COACH The person who runs a team's training program, working with the manager

COPA AMERICA CUP First won in 1910. North and South American national teams compete for the trophy every two years.

CORNER KICK A kick from the corner of the field, used to restart play when a member of the defending team has put the ball out of play over the goal line

CROSS A pass made from either wing to a forward at the center of the field

A referee's uniform

DEAD BALL KICK A kick from non-open play, such as a free kick or a corner kick

DERBY MATCH A game between two local rival teams

DIRECT FREE KICK A kick shot directly at the goal, awarded if a player kicks, trips, pushes, spits, or holds an opponent, or tackles the player rather than the ball

DIRECTORS The people who serve on a board to help run a team. Some invest their own money into the team.

DRIBBLING Running with the ball while keeping it under close control

EUROPEAN CUP First won in 1956, it is now known as the Champions League. The top clubs from the league of each European country compete for the trophy every year.

FA CUP First won in 1872. English league and non-league teams compete annually for the trophy.

FIFA The Federation Internationale de Football Association, the world governing body of soccer, formed in 1904; sets international rules, arbitrates between countries, and runs the World Cup

FOOTBALL ASSOCIATION The governing body of soccer for England, formed in 1863; arbitrates between clubs and disciplines players

A young player using his chest to control the ball

FORMATION The arrangement of the players on the field. The coach or manager chooses the formation and may change it during a game in response to the strengths or weaknesses of the opposition.

GIANT KILLER A team that beats a side believed to be of a much higher quality, and from a higher division

GLOVES Worn by goalkeepers to protect their hands and to help them grip the ball

GOAL KICK A kick from within the goal area, awarded when the ball goes out of play over the goal line and it was last touched by the attacking team

GROUNDSTAFF The people who look after the stadium, the terraces, and the soccer field

HANDBALL An offense occuring when a player touches the ball with the hands or arms during play

HEADING Hitting the ball with your head. A defensive header sends the ball up the field, clearing it as far away as possible. An attacking header sends the ball down the field, hopefully into the goal.

The white ball was introduced in 1951.

INDIRECT FREE KICK Awarded for dangerous play or for blocking an opponent. The player cannot score directly.

KICKOFF The kicking of the ball from the center point of the field to start the game.

LAWS FIFA's 17 Laws of the Game

MANAGER The person who picks the players, plans tactics, and decides what to do in training

MARKING Staying close to an opponent to prevent him from passing, shooting, or receiving the ball

MASCOT A person or animal that represents a team

OFFSIDE When an attacking player receives a ball, two defenders, including the goalkeeper, have to be between the attacking player and the goal. Otherwise, the attacker is offside. Players are only penalized for this if they interfere with play or gain some advantage by being in that position.

ONE-TWO In this move, an attacking player passes the ball to an advanced teammate and runs on into a space. The ball is immediately returned, bypassing the defending player.

PENALTY AREA A box that stretches 18 yards (16.5 m) in front of and to either side of the goal

PENALTY KICK A shot at goal from the penalty spot. Awarded against a team that commits an offense in its own penalty area.

PENALTY SPOT The spot 12 yards (13 m) in front of the goal. The ball is placed here to take a penalty.

PFA The Professional Footballers' Association; the trade union of football professionals in England and Wales that protects and promotes the interests of players

A collectible card

PHYSIOTHERAPIST (or PHYSICAL THERAPIST) The person who helps players recover from injuries using exercises, massage, and other treatments

PITCH The field of play. In the early days the boundaries of the pitch were marked by a series of flags. The FA introduced the pitch markings we know today in 1902.

PROGRAM A booklet providing information for the fans about the players of the teams in a particular game, as well as a message from the manager

RATTLE Supporters took rattles into soccer games until the 1960s, when they started to sing or chant instead. In most games, rattles are currently banned.

RED CARD Held up by the referee to indicate that a player has to leave the field. Serious foul play or two bookable offenses result in a red card.

REFEREE The person who has authority to enforce the rules during a particular match

SCARF Each team has a scarf in its own colors. Fans often wear the scarf or their team's colors when they go to games.

SCOUT A person employed by a team to look for talented new players and recruit them for the team

SET-PIECE A move practiced by a team to take advantage of a dead ball situation

SHIN PADS Pads worn inside socks to protect the lower legs

SHOOTING Kicking toward the goal

STANDS The areas where the supporters sit or stand around the field

STRIP The shirt, shorts, and socks a team wears. Most teams have at least two different strips, a home uniform and an away uniform. A team uses its away uniform when there is a conflict of colors.

STUDS (or CLEATS) Small rounded projections screwed into the sole of a soccer shoe The referee or assistant referee checks all studs before play starts. Players use longer studs on a wet, muddy field.

SUPERSTITIONS
Many players are deeply superstitious. For example, they may insist on wearing the same shirt number throughout their career. Paul Ince would only put on his shirt for a game as he ran out of the tunnel at the start of the match.

TACKLING Stopping an opponent who is in possession of the ball and removing the ball with your feet

TACTICS Planned actions or movements to achieve an advantage over your opponents

TERRACES Steps where people stood to watch a match before the advent of all-seat stadiums

THROW-IN A way of restarting play when the ball goes over the touchline; awarded to the opponent of the player who last touched the ball

World Cup medal

UEFA CUP Originally known as the Inter City Fairs Cup; first won in 1958. Some of the best teams from each European country's national league compete for the trophy every year.

WARM-UP A routine of exercises to warm up all the muscles before the start of a game

WHISTLE Used by the referee at the beginning and end of a match and to stop play when there is a foul

WINGER A striker who plays specifically on one side of the field or the other

WOMEN'S WORLD CUP First won in 1991. National women's teams compete for the trophy every four years.

WORLD CUP First won in 1930. National men's teams compete for the trophy every four years.

YELLOW CARD Held up by the referee to book a player

The United States Women's National Soccer Team, June 1998

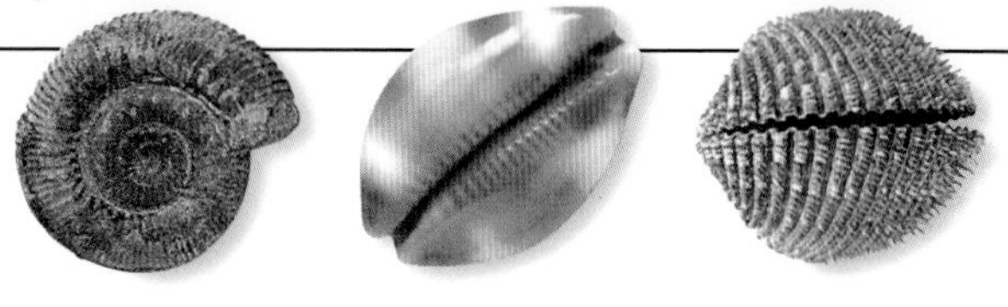

72-page Eyewitness Titles

American Revolution
Ancient Egypt
Ancient Greece
Ancient Rome
Arms & Armor
Astronomy
Baseball
Basketball
Bird
Castle
Cat
Crystal & Gem
Dance
Dinosaur
Dog
Early Humans
Earth
Explorer
Fish
Flying Machine
Food
Fossil
Future

Horse
Human Body
Hurricane & Tornado
Insect
Islam
Invention
Jungle
Knight
Mammal
Medieval Life
Mummy
Music
Mythology
NASCAR
North American Indian
Ocean
Olympics
Pirate
Plant
Pond & River

Pyramid
Religion
Rocks & Minerals
Seashore
Shakespeare
Shark
Shipwreck
Skeleton
Soccer
Space Exploration
Titanic
Tree
Vietnam
Viking
Volcano & Earthquake
Weather
Whale
Wild West
World War I
World War II

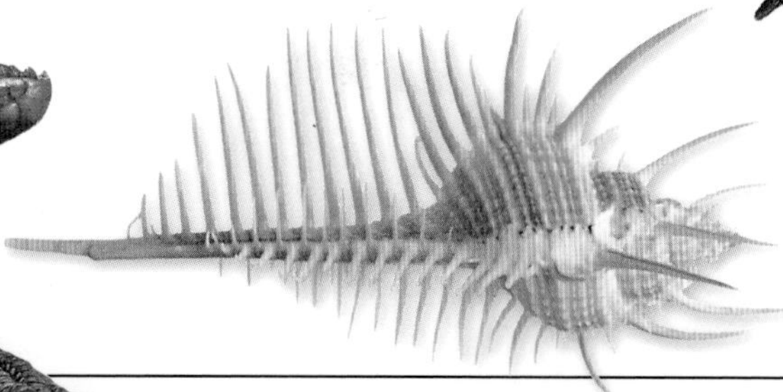

Other Eyewitness Titles

Index

Acknowledgments

The publisher would like to thank:
Hugh Hornby, Rob Pratten, Lynsey Jones, and Mark Bushell at The National Football Museum for their help and patience.

The publishers would also like to thank the following for their kind permission to reproduce their photographs:
(a=above; c=center; b=below; l=left; r=right; t=top; f=far; n=near)

Action Plus: 58bl; Glyn Kirk 15l, 18tr, 18cl, 18br, 19tl, 23cr, 44br, 51bl, 58clb; Matthew Clarke 19c; Neil Tingle 12br, 58-59; 62b.

Allsport: 34cl, 34br, 35tl, 35c; Ben Radford 58cr; Christopher Guibbaud 59tl; Claudio Villa 18bl;

Clive Brunskill 16bl; David Cannon 19c, 53cr; David Leah 53c; Don Morley 18br; Hulton Getty 36bl; Jed Jacbsohn 52c; Michael Cooper 59c; Michael King 36-7bc; Scott R Indermaur 45tl; Vincent Laforet 52br.

Associated Press AP: Alastair Grant 65tr.

Bryan Horsnell: 44cl, 44cfl, 44cnl.

Colorsport: 13tr, 21r, 23br, 29tr, 30tr, 34bl, 41tr, 46-7 b, 59tr, 62tl; Jerome Provost 41bc; Olympia 36br, 37tr.

Corbis UK Ltd: S Carmona 46clb.

Empics Ltd: 34tnr; Don Morley 37tr; Michael Steele 43bl, 43br; Neale

Simpson 40cl; Peter Robinson 36tc, 49l, 59br; Tony Marshall 19bl; Topham Picturepoint 36bc, 37tl; Witters 34tr; Matthew Ashton 62-63; Jon Buckle 64-65; Laurence Griffiths 63tl, 63ca; Peter Robinson 61clb.

FIFA: 62cb; 62br.

Getty Images: 60ca; 60cr; 61tr, Shaun Botterill 60-61, David Cannon 61cla, Jonathan Daniel 65br, Stu Forster 58cra; 61br, Gary M. Prior 60tr, Jamie Squire 59tcl.

Hulton Getty: 19bl; 35cr, 35bl, 36tl.

Mark Leech: 45bl.

Popperfoto: 53cl; 60bl; 62cl.

Rex Features: NWI 58bl.

Sporting Pictures (uk) Ltd: 4cr, 24cl, 25tl, 25tr, 33br, 38bl, 46cl.

Jacket images:
Front: Tc: Peter Robinson/EMPICS; Tcr: © Football Museum, Preston, UK; Tr: Actionplus Sports Images; B: Aflo Foto/Alamy. *Back:* DK Picture Library: The Football Museum (br, cla, c, clb, cra, tl, cr).

All other images
© Dorling Kindersley

For more information see:
www.dkimages.com